The SmartGirls Way

Strengths, Success, and Significance:
A Path for Women Entrepreneurs

By: Jean Brittingham and Tracey Ann Collins

© 2011 SmartGirls Way
All Rights Reserved.

No part of this book may be reproduced in any form by any electronic or mechanical means (including photocopying, recording, or information storage and retrieval) without permission in writing from the publisher.

Library of Congress Number:
ISBN 978-0-9838532-0-6

Cover illustrations © 2011 Jonathan Harris
Edited by: Sandy Chapman and Deborah Freeland
Interior design: Molly Charest

Visit us on the Web:
www.SmartGirlsWay.com

Published by:
SmartGirls Way Press
3440 E. Spruce Street
Seattle, WA USA 98122

Dedication

This book is dedicated to the wonderful women we interviewed for the book and the 100×100 Project. Your stories and advice are inspiring.

To my children, grandchildren, nieces, nephews, and the other beautiful young people who have inspired me to leave a world they can thrive in, and to Don for patience, Sarah for belief, and Lauralee for intention, and to Doug who always thought I had it in me, even when I wasn't sure.
— Jean

To my little sister and our children, Rowan, Liam, Caleb, Faye, and Eli. With special thanks to Greg, Bill, Claudia, and James: Without your help and support, this book would never have been written.
— Tracey

And to all the aspiring entrepreneurs, may this book help you launch your Vision-inspired Big Ideas and create your own lasting contribution to the world.

CONTENTS

Foreword ix
   Why This Book and Why Now x
   So How Do Women Respond? xi
   It's About Time xii
   The New Entrepreneur xii
   What You Will Find in *The SmartGirls Way* xiii
Chapter 1. Your Role in the *Next* Economy 1
   Why the World Needs Women Entrepreneurs 2
   Our Definition of "Entrepreneur" 4
   Underrepresentation of Women in Business Ownership 4
   Building an Inclusive Entrepreneurial Ecosystem 7
   The SmartGirls Way and You 9
   Choosing Your Path 11
Chapter 2. Where Nature Meets Nurture: The SGW Methodology . . 13
   Does the World Really Need Another Diagnostic? 14
   The SmartGirls Mirror in Brief 15
   SmartGirls Way Methodology 18
Chapter 3. Moving from Vision to Intention: The Vision Mind-Set . . 19
   Getting Started: Articulating Your ViBI 20
      Exercise 1: Articulating Your ViBI 20
   The Positive Mind-Set 23
Chapter 4. Interpreting the SmartGirls Mirror 29
   Interpreting Your SmartGirls Mirror 30
   The SmartGirls Mirror Characteristics 32
   Integrating Your SmartGirls Mirror 59
Chapter 5. SCAN 63
   See 64
   Connect 70
      Exercise 2: Creating Your Stakeholder Map 71

 Analyze 73
 Nest 74
Chapter 6. FOCUS. 77
 Find Your Relevancy 77
 Organize for Action 81
 Commit to Action 85
 Underwrite Yourself 90
 Start! 111
Chapter 7. THRIVE 115
 Trust 115
 Honesty 118
 Responsibility 122
 Intention 124
 Values 125
  Exercise 3: Defining Your Values 127
  Exercise 4: Prioritizing Your Values 127
 Empowerment 128
Chapter 8. Not-So-Final Words 131
 Skills for Successful Bridge Crossing 131
 New Habits 134
 Significance, Success, and Legacy 135
 Be Defined by Momentum 139
Chapter 9. Real SmartGirls Way Stories 140
 Elizabeth Bennett 141
 Michelle King Robson 143
 Ce Ce Chin 144
 Janice Shade 146
 Sarah McIlroy 148
 Amra Tareen 150
 Gretchen Schauffler 152
 Heidi Ganahl 154
 Stephanie Allen 156
 Jane Hoffer 157
 Sheryl O'Loughlin 159
 Sharon Lechter 162
Notes 165

Bibliography & Resources................................ 173
Additional Works Consulted 178
Online Resources 180
Glossary 182
Index 189
About the Authors 193

Foreword

Around five years ago, I became obsessed with the idea that women could make a huge impact on the way that businesses and the world were run if we could only embrace and leverage the ways in which we are different from men.

At the time, I—and many other women I knew—were being called to intervene in the largely negative paradigms we were observing at work and in the world. I had been involved for more than fifteen years in a sustainability practice that bridged government, business, and academia, where I intentionally sought to understand this call to action in terms of what is happening to the **triple bottom line**—planet, people, and profit.

The deeper I dug, the more I became convinced that my instincts were right: Women could make a huge difference if our ways of thinking, solving, and deciding were in balance with the masculine perspective. I also became convinced that *fighting* the established patriarchal culture would be exhaustive and ultimately not successful. Instead, I saw a need to create a culture that sits aside the existing one and is imbued with feminine memes: an analogous group of cultural ideas, norms, and practices that can be shared, learned, and acculturated with the powers and strengths of women in mind.

I became particularly enthralled with women entrepreneurs and the opportunities for women-owned businesses to influence multiple and mighty realms—politics, labor practice, health and wellness, and the role of nurturing in society, to name a few. I began interviewing and studying women entrepreneurs, looking for the common set of attributes that had helped them succeed, and in particular, looking for the "slip" factor—the point at which women give up their feminine approaches to problems because of the pressure of the more dominant win/lose culture of the masculine mind.

As the primary traits of successful women entrepreneurs emerged, another pattern revealed itself as well. These are the same traits needed to shift us to a sustainable and *thriving* existence on our planet, and not surprisingly, they are the traits talked about extensively in sustainability salons, environmental blogs, and even wonky policy meetings.

Why This Book and Why Now

While women have made tremendous strides in achieving gender parity *within* businesses, the fact remains that women are dramatically missing from the top positions of all professions. In corporate America, less than 4 percent of all chief executive officers are women. Even in those expert and technical professional careers in which women now surpass the number of men with graduate degrees—medicine, law, engineering, and management—their numbers drop off dramatically as you approach the top leadership and strategy positions of any organization.[1]

Some part of this does undoubtedly stem from women's desire to start and raise families. This in turn requires more flexibility and (in current corporate culture) often results in less responsibility. Yet not all women want—or choose—this path. In many cases, the reasons that women hesitate to return to the workplace have less to do with their children than with what I call "dis-ease" with the workplaces to which they are returning.

In nearly all cases, women will be returning to work environments where the culture is (intentionally or not) designed to undervalue the way they *communicate, work with others, accomplish goals,* and *achieve*. The intensely masculine culture of the business world with its *losers/winners, dog-eat-dog,* and *dominate-at-any-cost* ethos doesn't really work for most women. Interestingly, it doesn't really work for men, either. And it clearly is not working well for the world. Financial analysts and social scientists alike believe that the prevalence of this cultural paradigm is behind the greed and hubris at the heart of our current economic and environmental meltdown.

Although the recent recession has spurred a greater awareness of the value of female leadership in corporate America, the governance and management structure of this environment remains very masculine in its design and implementation, and it doesn't work for many, many women.

So How Do Women Respond?

We job-shop and seek paths to the top by adopting the ways of the dominant culture, all the while multitasking and agonizing over work/life balance. As a result, we more and more often fulfill our inherent and natural needs through our other lives—the lives that exist outside of our profession.

In other words, we reserve our passion for something besides our work!

But sometimes, we take the big and scary leap and activate our passion to start our own businesses.

There are a number of reasons I would like to see more of this, but the primary one is that the world needs women entrepreneurs if we are going to create the next economy successfully. The challenges of the coming decades require new business models that work better for new generations of workers. And by "next economy," I'm talking about a post-industrial world where technology, new business models, and new generations of workers converge. By our very nature, women entrepreneurs are uniquely positioned to shape and drive the next economy. We need women entrepreneurs.

› We need their great ideas in the marketplace.
› We need their products and services that are very aligned with the way the world needs to evolve.
› We need their know-how and well-honed sense of what works for families and communities.
› We need the kind of empowered, healthy companies they will create.
› And we need their influence in the broad landscape that the business community can affect—in everything from political leadership to responsible environmental and social stewardship.

So why hasn't the world jumped at the opportunity to capitalize on the benefits of women's intelligence? The answers lie within the current entrepreneurial ecosystem, in which access to capital, mentoring, talent, infrastructure, and customers comprise the life-support systems that feed individuals, organizations, and institutions.

It's About Time

There is no reason that such a vast number of good ideas and wealth should go untapped. This is where *The SmartGirls Way* begins.

The SmartGirls Way is a concept whose time has come and whose audience is broad. It is a methodology for understanding and leveraging the entrepreneurial strengths that define a way of *thinking, working,* and *interacting* for women who want to lead an economic revival that supports great businesses, families and communities, and a healthy planet now and into the future.

The tools and processes in this book are designed for:

> Women entrepreneurs

> Women who are wondering if they have what it takes to be successful business owners

> Men seeking a way to engage more effectively with the women they work with

> Investors seeking ways to understand and help women entrepreneurs

> Women who want to drive entrepreneurial change within their existing organizations

> Girls who want something different

> The fathers, spouses, partners, and friends who want that for them

The New Entrepreneur

Our definition of an entrepreneur is *not* the stereotypical approach where one takes on venture capital against an unlikely bet and works horrific and thankless hours (the thanklessness comes mostly from the venture-capital partners but also from the team you are driving and the family you are deserting) to break through the probability factor and post an amazing *win*—or at least get a buyout so that you break even.

This isn't *the* entrepreneur typology; it's *one* entrepreneur typology. However, we strongly believe that the state of the planet, the state of the economy, and the state of our lives, coupled with the incredible number of human beings who have great ideas they are turning into great businesses—make this stereotypical approach very limiting for women, and it's not going to help us build the next economy.

One of the most interesting aspects of the women entrepreneurs we interviewed is the motivation behind their ventures. Essentially, we're talking about a new breed of entrepreneur—where a much higher proportion of women are striking out and making a *difference* while making a *living*. These social entrepreneurs are developing businesses that offer solutions and hope because they see themselves and their business ideas as integral parts of a *better world*.

What You Will Find in *The SmartGirls Way*

While there have been many books written about (and indeed whole industries developed around) the differences between men and women, there is little to be found about how to *maximize* these differences to create more successful and empowered female business leaders. Instead of justifying (*Yeah, I'm different, and there's nothing wrong with that!*) or mitigating the effect of our gender discrepancies (*I cannot cry in a difficult business meeting!*), we should harness and embrace the unique qualities that comprise women's notable business intelligence.

In traditional business settings, we have worked to limit the idea that women are different because those differences have been used to disqualify us from the most important, strategic, and interesting roles. The content of our particular character has most often been deemed too soft for the boardroom.

The purpose of this book is to turn that notion on its head—to help our entrepreneurs and business leaders understand and leverage the core intelligence that is women's wisdom. Our goal is to help women recognize their strengths at work and in their lives, learn to intentionally develop the capacity to tap these amazing gifts, and most important, use this new knowledge to empower and energize their greatest dreams.

Specifically, we want to help women use their natural propensity to be passionate and intuitive communicators and problem solvers to *create and build the businesses they want to own*. The SmartGirls Way outlines how to use a woman's business intelligence (the way she thinks, feels, and communicates) to create her unarticulated business and implement her life strategy.

This book lays out important insights in three critical areas:

1. How women think and act
2. How these "ways of being" work in business
3. How you can leverage your feminine strengths to achieve your goals and in particular build the professional practice and business of your dreams

The SmartGirls Way is more than just a book about how women will help shape the next economy. It is also a tool to help you define your own SmartGirls Way profile and ultimately your dream business or career. Our goal is to help you identify and maximize your inherently female strengths, while providing pragmatic support and guidance in the form of inspiring stories and lessons learned from a community of successful entrepreneurs.

Most important, *The SmartGirls Way* explores the possibility that the differences between men and women can be celebrated—not just in relationships and family, but in business and society as a whole. We believe that by harnessing what makes women unique as individuals—and as businesspeople—we can deliver major benefits to society at a time when new insights and approaches are needed more than ever before.

Your Role in the *Next* Economy

Women think differently than men. It's well documented and ... we just *know* it. We discuss it, joke about it, and worry about it more than we really should. But very seldom do we celebrate and embrace our way of thinking in the business world.

There is no doubt that women have achieved many rights and accompanying freedoms over the past fifty years, yet we continue to view and evaluate ourselves, our behavior, and our opportunities through the eyes of a predominantly male-dominated culture.

The vast majority of women who *do* make it to the top echelons of our industries and enterprises all too often find themselves thinking and acting in ways that are counterintuitive to their very nature. So they try to train themselves to avoid those ways of thinking and behaving that are perceived as womanly, thereby diminishing opportunities to leverage the specifically feminine strengths that can fundamentally transform not only our own businesses but also future global economies and markets.

According to a 2004 Center for Advocacy study by the **Small Business Association (SBA)**, women represent nearly 47 percent of the U.S. labor force, yet own less than 14 percent of businesses that have employees.[1] Still, there is reason to be optimistic. Many economists and futurists believe that women represent the greatest untapped potential for economic growth through new-business incubation, representing significant new resources for economic recovery and a powerful source of sustainable growth.[2]

Studies have also shown that the social impact produced by women-owned businesses is disproportionately positive compared with companies owned by male entrepreneurs.

> › Women-owned businesses employ women at a higher rate and provide more services and flexibility to support family continuity than non-women-owned businesses.[3]

> Compared to men, women who own their own businesses will put more of their earned income back into their businesses or families.[4]
> Women-owned businesses generate other women-owned businesses, because the majority of women receive their capital and other essential support from other businesswomen.[5]

So why don't more women succeed as entrepreneurs? The barriers are both personal and societal. At a personal level, women often lack the confidence and resources to take that first step. They cite a fear of going into debt, or a lack of knowledge about how to write a business plan or obtain financing. And they crave support in the form of advice and guidance.[6]

On a social level, the obstacles are more onerous and will require a significant shift not only in the way women plan and implement their businesses but also in the current systems of support for entrepreneurs.

Why the World Needs Women Entrepreneurs

The political and economic events of the past decade have birthed a number of new academic, political, and philosophical macro-trends affecting the future of society. Two of these directly correlate with women's role in the future—and in particular the need for increased female leadership in business: **sustainability** and the **next economy**.

In the context of this book, when we refer to *sustainability,* we are talking about the immediate need to acknowledge and act upon the truth that human society survives only because of the ecosystem that supports our needs. This includes nature and all of its complex interactions that provide us with air, water, energy, food, and processes for disposing of our waste materials. It is no longer debatable that we are overwhelming and confounding the Earth's capacity to do its job. The question is, how can we possibly mitigate the suffering of future generations if we do not *now* begin to act synergistically with nature? In his book *Ishmael*, Daniel Quinn aptly summarizes this tension between civilization and the conditions that govern irrefutable laws like gravity:[7] You don't have to like the laws, they just work anyway.[8] In this vein, sustainability is essentially *meeting the needs of today's society without making it impossible for future generations to also enjoy life on Planet Earth.*

In terms of the *next economy*, we are talking about economic vitality within the framework of the system conditions mentioned above and the ability to overcome the "disease of short-termism" that has contributed to the recent economic crisis. In his book *Capitalism as if the World Matters,* Jonathon Porritt raises a driving question: "How will millions of people live and work in a complex business environment that eliminates suffering, increases quality of life, and protects our 'life-support' systems?"[9]

Many experts believe that we will design ourselves into this world only under duress; but ultimately, the industrial world must be replaced with what sustainability activist Paul Hawken calls "human-centered enterprises that are sustainable producers." We agree with Hawken's theory that "ecology offers a way to examine all present economic and resource activities from a biological—rather than a monetary—point of view that can lead us to a restorative economy."[10]

The exhausting effect of greed-driven bubbles, followed by the precipitous falls that have plunged world economies and millions of families into crisis, coupled with the increasing threat to the very systems that support life on our planet, all collide to make a crystal clear case for a new approach to economic vitality: *We need to do something different.*

More than ever before, society needs the shift that a significant influx of successful female entrepreneurs, business owners, and leaders can bring. And we have never been more prepared for—indeed, we have never longed for more—the significant opportunity that awaits us.

That opportunity is, as Riane Eisler suggests in her latest work, *The Real Wealth of Nations*, to create a genuinely *caring economy*—one based on balance and a respect for the intricate relationships that keep our planet and society healthy.[11] We will not find a workable path to the future or effectively reset economic and social stability until we do so.

Taken together with the increasing strain we have put on our planet—a planet with finite resources and abilities to process our waste—the required shift becomes not just welcome, not just necessary, but *critical* and *urgent*.

Luckily for the world, women are ready to step up. What matters to women crosses every political and ideological line. While we may not always agree with each other's politics, we're going to come together on some very basic ways of being, those ways that matter most to us: how we care for our families and communities.

We care about how the decisions we make affect others, and how the decisions that are made on our behalf are going to affect those we love and care about. We're intuitive, passionate, and creative. We understand the implications of decisions for our families, our business, and for the future. These inherently female attitudes and characteristics are the basis for defining the role women will play in the reframing that is necessary for sustainable economic recovery.

Our Definition of "Entrepreneur"

SmartGirls Way **entrepreneurs** are women with **Vision-inspired Big Ideas (ViBIs)** who use *intuition, creativity,* and *personal integrity* to build thriving businesses. By balancing curiosity, passion, and a unique ability to weave together community, ideas, and networks, a SmartGirl will build a successful business that fuels the next economy and in doing so will make the world a better place.

She may be the small-business owner looking to expand or grow her business, a solo entrepreneur looking to expand a passion or hobby into a viable opportunity, or a social entrepreneur creating a better way to engage and support communities across the globe. By definition, because she is accountable for risks and outcomes, a SmartGirl can also be an entrepreneur within her organization or community.

Essentially, we're talking about a new breed of entrepreneur, where the complexities of our society, environment, and lifestyles converge. There are many, many women out there who fit this model, and this new entrepreneur can have a tremendous impact on our economy if we can overcome some specific barriers.

Underrepresentation of Women in Business Ownership

Women outnumber men on the planet. We have the right in every corner of the developed world to vote, and our right to work and receive equal pay for equal effort is protected by law. We are as interested in financial security as men (more so in many cases) and the recent **Great Recession**[12] has resulted in nearly 40 percent of women with children becoming the primary breadwinners in their households.[13] Since the 1980s, women have outnumbered men in most fields of study for undergraduate degrees. In 2010, the number of women obtaining PhDs surpassed men, and we are closing the gap in doctorate degrees awarded to women in engineering and mathematics.[14] Women are the acknowledged decision makers in a consumption-driven economy. Paying attention to how women think, what we care about, and what we therefore might buy is the basis of much of our *trillion-dollar* marketing and advertising industry.

With numbers like this, why isn't the world a more caring, connected, compassionate, and future-focused place? Where are the women leaders in business ownership, corporate governance, and the political and policy-creation circles?

A deeper look at the numbers tells the rest of the story in terms of real financial security, independence, and influence. To an alarming degree, the global business and political landscape is still dominated by men. The world of ultimate decision making is dramatically overbalanced in favor of the ways of men. In fact, it's pretty frustrating how little progress has really been made.

› In the last U.S. midterm election, women achieved the highest proportion of seats ever held in Congress and the Senate—*16 percent*—yet the United States ranks *sixty-ninth* among countries with women in government.[15]

› Although women are now equal to men in advanced degrees, they still lag behind by nearly *20 percent* in pay for the same jobs.[16]

› Even in those expert and technical professional careers—medicine, law, engineering, and management—in which women have made tremendous progress, at the point they graduate from college, they comprise only *22 percent* of the total number of graduates, and their numbers drop off dramatically as they approach the top leadership and strategy positions of any organization.[17]

› In Silicon Valley, for every *one hundred* shares of stock options owned by a man, only *one* share is owned by a woman.[18]

› Only *3 percent* of Fortune 500 companies are led by women CEOs.[19]

› Women represent less than *20 percent* of the overall U.S. labor force working in executive leadership positions.[20]

Some of the liability for the lack of women in senior positions undoubtedly has to do with a woman's desire to have and raise a family and the need therefore for more flexibility, which often translates (in current corporate culture) to less business responsibility. The so-called "mommy track" is in fact, in most cases, more like a permanent derailment.

Women who make the choice in the United States to nurture and care for their children in the early critical years are often forced by corporate norms to choose between thriving and robust families or successful careers. Even in those places where there is an official policy of "on-ramping" women who have been off for significant breaks to nurture their families, they have to work three times as hard (they were already working twice as hard) as their male peers to catch up. If not completely derailed, they are put years behind on their career paths.

Yet for most of the women we've interviewed, their hesitation in returning to the workplace has less to do with children per se and more to do with their general unease in returning to workplaces that make them choose between *life* and *work, collaborate* and *compete,* and *learn* and *climb.*

When women do return to work because they must support families or are passionate about what they are doing, they are often restless and unsatisfied. It's not just a matter of missing their children at home. Nor is it a disconnect in how women view their role in caring for children in the context of the future success of our societies. It's much deeper than that. Workplaces just don't work for them anymore. And it's important to note that they don't work for many women who are not now and never plan to be mothers. It's not just about nurturing. It's about being female.

In her book *The Female Brain,* Louann Brizendine describes how from the beginning girls are hardwired (and encouraged) to communicate, collaborate, and create community.[21] We have a tremendous opportunity to harness this inherently female programming as now, more than ever before in modern history, our world is rapidly changing to one where understanding and being able to navigate complex and interrelated constellations of relationships is not only a key to success, but the key to the future.

In recent years, the soft skills (building relationships, communicating, collaborating) associated with the female half of the population have been gaining credibility and merit in the business world as the **Emotional Intelligence (EI) quotient**—a term intended to bring understanding and focus to emotional capabilities as "IQ" does for intelligence. Some corporations are even stepping up to train organizational leaders to think and behave with a more balanced EI mentality. Unfortunately, to equalize these two mind-sets, many sociologists and historians from academia to the United Nations agree that there remains one gigantic social barrier: the often invisible cultural constructs and behaviors around **sexism**.

Sociologist Gerda Lerner argues that subordination of women precedes all other subordinations and that to rid ourselves of all of the other "isms"—racism, classism, ageism, and so forth—it is sexism that must first be eradicated.[22]

To do this, we need a movement. Women know there is a better way. There is a better way than giving up and adopting the ways of the dominant culture. There is a better way for women to seek fulfillment of their inherent and natural needs through their businesses instead of having to find it in their lives outside of work.

> There is a different way—a better way. The SmartGirls Way!

We'd like to help these women face their fears, overcome barriers, and learn to navigate the waters to successful entrepreneurship.

Building an Inclusive Entrepreneurial Ecosystem

In her book *Women Lead the Way,* Linda Tarr-Whelan highlights the social impact of the "30% solution," essentially the value, richness, and diversity that occur when 30 percent of any group is comprised of a minority. Tarr-Whelan also points to the disproportionately positive impact produced by women-owned businesses compared with companies owned by male entrepreneurs.[23]

Women have endless enthusiasm, energy, discipline, and dedication, and—as outlined earlier in this chapter—empowered women represent the greatest potential for redefining the economic landscape and possibilities for new-business creation. In fact, according to the most recent estimates of the number, employment, and revenues of women-owned firms, women are starting new businesses at nearly twice the rate of men in the United States and in 2010 accounted for 29 percent of all enterprises. However, they employ only 6 percent of the country's workforce and produce approximately 4 percent of business revenues.[24]

To shift this disproportionate ratio and truly be successful, we need to overcome some of the barriers that lie within the existing entrepreneurial ecosystem: access to capital, mentors, talent, affordable business-support services, markets, and customers.

Just as the ecosystem of the planet provides a critical set of services for life on Earth, the same applies to the term *ecosystem* taken out of that biological environment. Ecosystems are interdependent and symbiotic. In other words, while some services can be provided outside of the ecosystem, when any part is missing, the overall effectiveness of the system is decreased.

There are essential ingredients within an entrepreneurial ecosystem to support and encourage the innovation, incubation, and risk taking

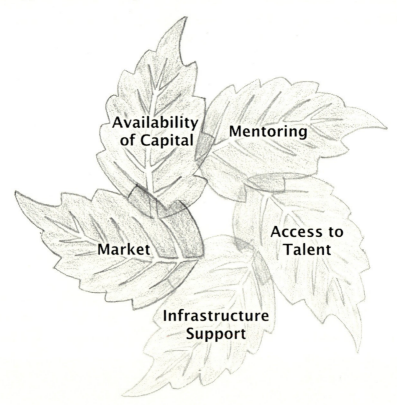

Ecosystem of Women Entrepreneurs

of entrepreneurship. When one or two of these elements are there, they may fill necessary elements but will not be sufficient for rapid and robust scaling of new businesses.

In addition to the ecosystem elements listed above, women entrepreneurs typically will need to create an effective and strong community of support. We address this specifically in the chapters to come, but it is worth mentioning here, as it applies to the business world: *If any one aspect of the ecosystem is missing, the necessary resources for starting and scaling a business are more difficult to acquire.*

Through their commitment to network, learn, and understand the requirements for businesses to thrive, many women are already finding success. By increasing access to the ecosystem services, filling gaps, and creating platforms and tools to connect the ecosystem elements, we believe that many more women will not only start businesses, but also scale those businesses to achieve significant economic growth. The businesses these women run will help define, shape, and ensure the success of the next economy.

The SmartGirls Way and You

While there have been many books written and indeed whole industries developed around the differences between men and women, little has been written about how to take these differences and do more than superficially celebrate them. The SmartGirls Way is not about celebrating differences—it's about leveraging them.

Instead of teaching you how to impersonate male entrepreneurs, the SmartGirls Way outlines a methodology for activating your unique qualities and turns them into a powerful tool for building the business you want to own. We want you to recognize your unique strengths at work and in your life, learn to intentionally develop the capacity to tap these amazing gifts, and, most important, use this new knowledge to practically and confidently realize those dreams.

By writing this book, we aim to help you systematically and confidently approach launching, building, and scaling your business. The SmartGirls Way Methodology provides a framework and disciplined approach to creating value as well as attracting investment and revenue that can result in profit, growth, and success.

Most women (and many men) possess the attributes discussed in this book—attributes that are necessary for us to accomplish the massive changes that will be needed for society to thrive into the future. As we've mentioned, there are many questions to answer about how 9 billion people can live in relative peace and prosperity on one small planet. It will take a lot of ingenuity and new models of commerce. It will take a different approach to markets and customer satisfaction—an honest and accountable free-market economy that balances capitalism with the needs of the planet.

Every woman reading this book and thinking about starting a business that works *with* and *for* her instead of fighting her authentic self has something in common with every other woman. At the heart of this book is this one single idea: *All the wisdom necessary for your success is out there in the community of women*. For generations, women have been the keepers of community. We have tended, nurtured, and enhanced our communities by sharing our stories and supporting one another. This same sense of community is an essential thread throughout the entrepreneurial ecosystem, and to nurture it, we need to nurture one another by sharing success stories and building "smart networks" with other women.

We can help, you can help yourself, and we can help each other to build better lives, a better economy, and a more robust, balanced world.

Throughout this book, we have included stories of successful women (spanning all stages of businesses across many industries) who, in the spirit of the SmartGirls Way, have leveraged their strengths to overcome challenging times and barriers to growth.

These stories illustrate the core of the **SmartGirls Mirror**—a strengths-assessment diagnostic introduced in the next chapter. The Mirror provides insights in three critical areas:

1. How women think and act in business, and where and why it works
2. How your particular SmartGirls Mirror will apply to your business
3. How these SmartGirls characteristics can serve as your anchor for reaching your business goals, building your professional success, and building the business of your dreams

Once you have completed the diagnostic, we have created tools to help you:
- › Identify your own SmartGirls characteristics
- › Create strategies to hone and use these skills effectively
- › Understand how to recognize and shift conversations that put women's ways and intelligences in question
- › Define your intention and plot a course to realize your dream business or career

Choosing Your Path

At the heart of the SmartGirls Way lies a pivotal question. The answer to this question becomes the central axis that grounds your strengths as you build your business.

How does your dream make sense as a business?

As much as any model, book, mentor, or process can give you guidance and support to answer the subsequent questions to shape and scale your business, this central creative act is *all you*. It has to be yours. You have to commit to it. And you must believe in it!

The evolution of your concept into a business is where dream meets reality. It is also where opportunity meets practicality. Most important, it is where *passion* meets *action*.

Passion without a course can certainly heat up a meeting, a dinner conversation, or a social-network exchange, but it rarely (if ever) really changes anything. It represents raw energy and undirected desire. It is often inflamed from a sense of fear, a lack of equity or access, or even just a sense that something *could* and *should* be done.

Big ideas are great, but they are just dreams unless you can put energy into them and keep them from doing what dreams tend to do—fade back into the subconscious to either disappear forever or inform some other idea for the future.

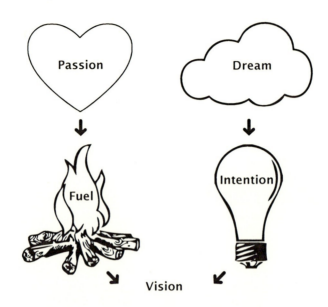

When Action Meets Passion

On the other side of this equation, if you can commit to your dream and begin applying discipline to your passion, something quite amazing happens—you begin to shape the future.

When your dream becomes an intention and your passion becomes fuel, your vision is born. Your commitment to shape your dream into a business may be the best promise you ever make to yourself. We can help you navigate the most direct path to success. It won't be easy, and it's not about reading the book. It's about keeping this idea in front of you.

It's your dream, and it's yours to make real.

If you are ready for the adventure, let's get started.

Where Nature Meets Nurture: The SmartGirls Way Methodology

Opinions on the role of nature and nurture in women's entrepreneurship could fill an entire book. In fact, one of the least discussed realities of modern society is that gender inequity remains a global issue, and male privilege and dominance have been written into nearly every religion and code of conduct in the world today.[1]

But this book is not about *that*; it is about *you*. And we are not here to create a new battle over differences or privilege. What this book *is* about is the role that nature has played in preparing you to be an excellent entrepreneur and the equally important role that nurturing will play in the inception, growth, and success of your business.

Women have been endowed with a good deal of natural capability and strong preferences for certain behaviors and characteristics. In general terms, we are comfortable with communication. We have an ability to understand and track many issues at once. We are empathetic and perceptive to the social sensitivities and needs of others. We have a constant and almost unlimited ability to make connections between ideas and solutions. Over time, women have nurtured, developed, and mastered these behaviors to the point that they are recognizable characteristics.

Among all of the characteristics of women are unique strengths that women entrepreneurs possess. After conducting over two hundred interviews with successful women over the past three years, we've identified six characteristics that can very much contribute to a woman's way of entrepreneurship. These strengths are **Integrity**, **Creativity**, **Intuition**, **Passion**, **Curiosity**, and **Weaving**. When honed and consistently applied, these strengths work together to bring success and fulfillment through entrepreneurship.

We all possess these characteristics to some degree, and they are the heart of the SmartGirls Mirror, a diagnostic tool designed to help you understand and leverage these characteristics as you dream, launch, and grow your business. In entrepreneurship, as in life, when we focus on our strengths, we set our sights on learning and growing, and we reveal our best abilities and what comes most naturally to us.

The diagnostic is therefore a starting point to help you build from strength to strength, hone and remain focused on your key business or idea, build confidence, and then master behaviors and skills that help your business launch, scale, and thrive.

Does the World Really Need Another Diagnostic?

By the time you reach maturity in modern Western society, you have typically been exposed to a number of ways of grading, dividing, and categorizing yourself. Some of this is useful measurement and can give you the ability to be more effective in society. Much of this measurement is meant to help others simplify, organize, and classify types of people for business and educational hierarchies. In some cases, measurement tools help us to illuminate distinctions that are useful for self-improvement and organizing effective workgroups or teams. Many of these "tests"—if taken thoughtfully—can be helpful and insightful, but for women, they can be incomplete because they do little if anything to provide a look into the *differences* in the ways that women and men think, feel, and act in their day-to-day lives.

When these insights are provided, it is nearly always in the context of relationships—how to better understand each other and make your relationships happier and more robust. This can be a worthy focus and needed by many, but knowing that men are from another planet or have a "nothing" box isn't going to help us much in building our businesses or reaching the *other* goals we have in life beyond a healthy relationship.

As women who want to create and build great relationships *and* families *and* businesses *and* futures, we need to know a lot more about how to work *from our strengths*.

The SmartGirls Mirror in Brief

The SmartGirls Mirror is a self-assessment tool that measures your particular strengths in six core areas to help you understand how they inform—and then actualize—your vision. The Mirror can also help you to identify your blind spots. For example, what happens to your Passion or Curiosity when you don't know how to leverage these strengths to build your business?

Applied in the context of a SmartGirls Way approach, the Mirror and supporting exercises and methods can help you:

› Close your gaps
› Maximize and leverage your strengths to amplify your other characteristics
› Understand how to modify your starting point based on your core strength
› Dream big as you gain the confidence to scale successfully

The diagnostic and descriptions of each characteristic will also help you assess:

› Your ability to overcome the "yes, buts"
› Your willingness to hold on to an idea
› Your readiness to grow *with* your idea as it shapes into a business

The SmartGirls Way begins with your Vision-inspired Big Idea (or ViBI). It may not yet be fully grown, but this is the seed inside you that you will grow by magnifying your strengths. We should also point out the obvious and intended metaphorical meaning of the SmartGirls Mirror. Women are often self-critical, and in life and business, we have a tendency to focus on our weaknesses rather than our strengths. The SmartGirls Mirror is intended to break that habit, and instead reflect a consistent portrait of strengths. Because being authentic to your inner strengths is paramount in entrepreneurial success, it is very much our intention that when you look in the SmartGirls Mirror, you will love the reflection looking back at you.

Within the Mirror are the six SmartGirls characteristics that are defined by a woman's own character. The central characteristics—Intuition,

Creativity, and Integrity—are closest to your vision. These are the internal checkpoints that will propel your ViBI into motion.

Internal Strengths

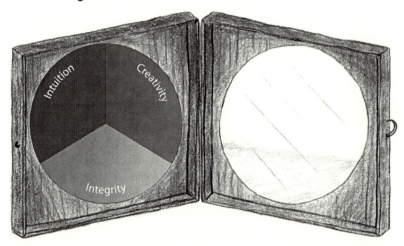

Women have biologically and historically developed traits that allow them to nurture and are therefore very concerned with equity, fairness, and balance. We call this *Integrity*, and it impacts everything from equity among your employees to the relationships you forge with your partners and customers, and ultimately the role of female-owned businesses in the next economy. In the world of sustainable entrepreneurship, Integrity is often the catalyst that sparks our vision and feeds our Passion.

When we talk about "woman's Intuition" (*we know what we know*), we do so while acknowledging that women haven't always been encouraged to recognize their strong intuitive knowledge. In the SmartGirls world, woman's Intuition isn't just a notion—it's a strength to be reckoned with!

Creativity is a critical ingredient for any entrepreneur. We all have some element of Creativity, and as entrepreneurs, we apply this skill to explore the outer limits and infinite possibilities of our business.

Curiosity, Passion, and Weaving are the external characteristics that explore how your business fits with your life, your community, and the world. We refer to these three characteristics as the "amplifier" strengths because they are most often the strengths you employ in your external engagements with others.

External Strengths

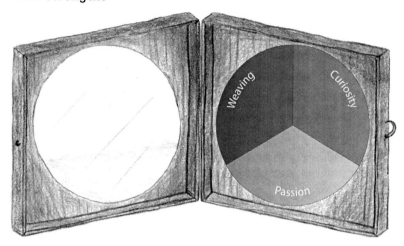

When we focus our natural Curiosity to understand how our particular idea fits in the world, it propels us to seek out those ideas that are similar to our own. As women, our Curiosity acts as a strength when it forces us to dig deeper and continue to dig at something.

Passion is not just about caring deeply; it is about bringing the positive energy of emotion to fuel ideas that create not only great breakthroughs, but also the perseverance that separates a great *idea* from a great *business*.

Weaving is about networking, connecting, and juggling multiple ideas at once. As women, we are incredibly adept at threading behaviors and ideas together to create relationships and build community. When we weave, we create connections and patterns that motivate others to action and drive real change.

(We will explore these characteristics in depth in Chapter 4 and learn how they fit into the SmartGirls Way Methodology for your business.)

By thinking about your ViBI when responding to each question in the SmartGirls Mirror, you can keep alive that spark that motivated you to create your business, and you allow it to grow and expand its influence, not only on you, but also on the community and world it touches.

SmartGirls Way Methodology

The SmartGirls Mirror will also help illuminate your path as you grow your ViBI from the seed of an idea into a living, breathing business. As it grows, the SmartGirls Way Methodology leads you through three organic steps—**SCAN**, **FOCUS**, and **THRIVE**—for shaping your ViBI into the business you'd like to own. We will go through these steps after you have completed the diagnostic in Chapter 3. As you go through the steps, your SmartGirls Mirror can serve as the source of energy for nurturing and growing your business within the context of your life and marketplace.

Moving from Vision to Intention: The Vision Mind-Set

If you are reading this book, chances are you have an idea, dream, or vision for starting or scaling a business. At the inception stage, we call this the Vision-inspired Big Idea (ViBI). A SmartGirls ViBI doesn't have to be about changing the world—but it can have an *impact* on the world.

Before you take the diagnostic, you need to first identify and then articulate this ViBI to yourself. For Elizabeth Bennett, cofounder of Africa Direct, the ViBI for her African-craft importing business began as an extended trip to Africa with her family. The trip was meant to be an eight-month hiatus from Elizabeth's corporate career and a recently failed entrepreneurial venture. It was also meant to be a political and cultural experience for her three youngest children—all of whom were adopted African-Americans—to explore their ancestral roots.

While touring throughout Africa, Elizabeth and her family were struck by both the beauty of the crafts produced by local women artisans and the difficult conditions in which these women lived. They bought as many goods as they could, and by the time they were ready to leave Africa, they literally had a van full of crafts—many, many more than they really needed.

"I had no idea what I was going to do with everything we had acquired on our trip. I didn't have a job to go back to, nor did I have a real plan; but at an unconscious level there was an idea for a business," explains Elizabeth. "I felt that we could make a significant difference in the lives of these artisans if we could introduce them to an American market."

This sparked an idea for a business: How could she continue to bring these beautiful artifacts back to others in a way that would significantly support the artists in these villages *and* provide for her own family at the same time?

Soon thereafter, Elizabeth and her partner, Sara Luther, launched Africa Direct, but Elizabeth knew that to be a viable business for both the living artists in Africa and her family, she would need to quickly expand her market. Her **eureka moment** came when she decided to distribute her goods on eBay. "When your market hits you over the head, you're wise if you notice it. It was luck that eBay was just taking off at the time, and it was the missing piece for my vision."

Today, Africa Direct is one of the largest retailers of African-made products online and supports the economy of more than seventy villages.

In every single story we share with you in this book, a vision was formed, validated, incubated, and defined by a woman's own character. For any woman setting out as an entrepreneur, one of the most important things to do is understand how the things you're talking and dreaming about fit with your individual character and personal vision.

Getting Started: Articulating Your ViBI

To get started, you need to ask yourself some questions about your vision, dream, or big idea, and determine which stage of entrepreneurship you are in.

It helps if you can phrase your ViBI as an *intention* in a *question format*. No matter what entrepreneurial stage you are in, take the time to write down your ViBI, using the worksheet below in Exercise 1. Think about (1) your ViBI, (2) what you should be doing at *this* stage to bring your ViBI to fruition, (3) the reason you are inspired to move into the next stage of your ViBI, and (4) what, specifically, you would consider "success" in this stage. Read your answers out loud, first to yourself and then to someone close to you. When you share your intention with someone else, it becomes a catalyst for action.

Exercise 1: Articulating Your ViBI

My ViBI is:	①	
Intention statement:	②	
My entrepreneurial stage now: * ☐ Stage 1 ☐ Stage 2 ☐ Stage 3	Why do I want to do this? ③	How will I measure success? ④

Stage 1 is: I have a dream or a big idea that I am considering turning into a business. Stage 2 is: I am starting a new business. Stage 3 is: I want to scale/grow my business.

If you're having trouble capturing your ViBI, here is an example of how one woman's ViBI evolved out of her personal decision to make a difference.

EmpowHER founder Michelle King Robson started her company following her own personal struggle with a debilitating health issue that left her feeling hopeless and alone. In 2008, she launched EmpowHER as a new-media platform that provides women with the most comprehensive and up-to-date information available on women's health, as well as a forum for women to connect and share stories of struggle and hope. Michelle's business evolved from first building a world-class online platform for women and their health to amassing one of the largest women's-health libraries anywhere. The result is a secure, online, peer-to-peer social community for women to ask their health questions, share their stories, advocate for themselves, and advocate for others.

Looking back, Michelle credits her ability to create a strong team and that team's ability to connect with their community as the key drivers of her success: "We built something women wanted, and they've given us their approval by making us the fastest-growing, oft-visited women's health site on the Web. You're given permission to scale your business when you've earned the trust of your customers and partners. The rest follows."

Since then, she has taken a lead in health advocacy, heading the second-largest write-in campaign in FDA history for drugs and treatments for women's health. EmpowHER has won numerous awards and will reach more than 33 million women in 2011.

While Michelle's ViBI has been the root of her business, her *intention* for the business has grown and evolved in the past three years. Following is how Michelle would have completed her ViBI worksheet at each stage of her business.

Articulating Your ViBI –
Michelle King Robson, EmpowHER

My ViBI is:	How do I ensure that no woman ever suffers in silence like I did?	
Intention statement:	How do I launch a health-education and empowerment platform?	
My entrepreneurial stage now:	Why do I want to do this?	How will I measure success?
☑ Stage 1 I have a dream or a big idea that I am considering turning into a business.	I want to change the face of women's health around the world by empowering women to own their health and wellness, and to teach them how to best advocate for themselves and their loved ones.	When every woman regardless of socioeconomic status, geography, or race has access to all the health information, resources, tools, and support from a community of her peers to live her healthiest life.

Intention statement:	How do I attract the right media partners and talent to my company?	
My entrepreneurial stage now	Why do I want to do this?	How will I measure success?
☑ Stage 2 I am starting a new business.	Attracting and assembling the right team will be my first and most critical priority. Team and relationships are the foundation for success. With the right foundation, I know I will make it through whatever comes my way, make better decisions, and attract the right partners (investors, strategic relationships, clients, and others).	My team members are super-smart and possess world-class skills in their respective areas of responsibility. I will look at how deeply they connect to our company mission and with the lives of the women we impact every day. I will know I've succeeded in putting the right people on the bus when they connect to their work at a soul level, not just at a skill-set level.

Intention statement:	How do I scale and grow my business to continue our growth and reach the broadest number of women while creating a profitable business?	
My entrepreneurial stage now	Why do I want to do this?	How will I measure success?
☑ Stage 3 I want to scale/grow my business.	The importance of disciplined, prioritized, and focused growth cannot be overstated. I know I will be forced to make tough choices between wants, needs, and nice-to-haves all the time. Being honest with myself early and often about how to prioritize will keep me from making expensive mistakes.	I will know I have achieved scale when I can answer these questions: Have we built something women want? Are we growing every day? Are we attracting the major health and wellness brands we want to do business with us? Are the biggest traditional and digital media companies in the world seeking our partnership?

The Positive Mind-Set

One critical difference between someone with a really good idea and an entrepreneur is a simple way of looking at the world. Most of the time, someone comes up with an idea, and the response is, "Yes, but..."—and then a litany of reasons why the idea won't work. The visioning process is not the time to set limitations on yourself—there will be enough other people doing that for you down the road!

Over the years, we've encountered quite a few of these ways in which that women tend to stop themselves from reaching their greatest success. The top three we like to call the "Yes, but..." dream killers:

"**Yes, but...**"
...it's too hard.
...I don't see how I can make money doing this.
...it will require too big a sacrifice.

As women, we tend to fall prey to this anti-entrepreneurial mind-set more than men. A 2007 Global Entrepreneurship Monitor survey found that a reduced fear of failure among women in particular was an important predictor of successful entrepreneurship.[1] Is the underlying problem really a fear of failure, or an impossible standard of achievement by which we measure ourselves?

One way to eliminate this self-imposed mind-set is to imagine your business without limitations. Instead of saying "Yes, but...."—what if you said, "Yes, and...."? To help you convey this, we asked successful entrepreneurs to share their insights related to these myths.

1. It's too hard.

For fashion designer Ce Ce Chin, a positive mind-set was an important component in her decision to leave her successful career working with top designers such as Michael Kors and Calvin Klein to start 80%20 Shoes.

"You have to really think about what is motivating you to be an entrepreneur. For me, the financial potential wasn't as important as a desire to have creative control over my own designs," she explains. "It would have been too hard for me not to do this because I knew that if I didn't try I would carry that regret for the rest of my life."

Ce Ce readily admits that she didn't exactly know what she was getting into. She started working nights and weekends on her first design, a painted canvas slip-on shoe. She also sought support from her existing network, approaching retailers she knew from her accessory-designer days who would sell items on consignment.

One day, a writer at DailyCandy noticed Ce Ce's shoes and promptly wrote a story about them. The coverage from the fashion website resulted in such a large flood of emails inquiring about her shoes that Ce Ce was inspired to leave her full-time job to pursue her own company.

"I had no idea how I was going to manufacture the shoes. But I just knew that if didn't take a risk and start devoting a hundred percent of my time and energy to my own company, the momentum and energy would slip away," she says.

Like many women, Ce Ce had to weigh the risks between existing job security and living her dream. In the end, she didn't allow herself to be stymied by fear. "You have to be instrumental in creating those moments of inspiration; if you don't try something, you will never see the result."

2. I don't know how I will raise/make money.

When Janice Shade decided to follow her Intuition and leverage her extensive career in consumer packaged goods, she knew that less than 10 percent of companies that receive venture capital are owned or run by women. To launch her affordable, all-natural body product line, TrueBody Products, she cashed in her 401(k) and leveraged her credit cards, but she knew it wouldn't be enough; she'd have to bring in outside capital from somewhere. She sought advice from her former mentor and employer, and to her surprise, he became her first investor.

"I had no idea he'd be in a position to help me, but he was really passionate about getting socially responsible businesses funded," she says.

While Janice's unexpected encounter with an investor was ideal, the point was that she didn't allow her fear and uncertainty to prevent her from exploring every avenue. If she hadn't been committed to raising money, she would not have arranged for the meeting to seek her mentor's advice in the first place. We explore options for raising capital in Chapter 6; for now, the important takeaway is not to let uncertainty prevent you from taking the first step.

3. It will require too big a sacrifice.

Finally, we need to dispel this myth that entrepreneurs all have some kind of work ethos disease. Yes, it requires commitment and hard work to build a thriving business, but we strongly reject the notion of an entrepreneur as someone who abandons her personal life and makes choices that decrease her connections and *joie de vivre*. Indeed, we believe both you and your business can thrive and that you can enjoy your life *more* through the process of entrepreneurship.

As a child, Sarah McIlroy would spend hours with her mother creating clothing designs and sewing them together. When she started FashionPlaytes, a clothing company where girls design their own custom clothing, she did so because she wanted to create that same experience for her own children, and it became the seed for her ViBI.

"What little girl doesn't want to be a fashion designer and create something unique? I not only wanted to create this experience for my own children, I wanted every girl to have that opportunity," Sarah says.

So after years working in the gaming industry, she decided to leave her high-paying job and founded FashionPlaytes.com, which enables girls aged five to twelve years to design their own clothing. "I felt as if my whole career had led up to this moment, and I didn't want to look back ten years from now and see that someone else had done what I could do."

Sarah knew that starting a company wouldn't be easy, and she had to weigh the impact this new commitment would have on her family. "I was determined to have a meaningful experience in both worlds and try to strike a lifestyle balance," she says.

When a longtime mentor raised concerns about the timing of the economy and the energy required to nurture both a business and Sarah's three young children, she was faced with a decision.

"I felt his comments were condescending," she explains. "He insinuated that a mother with three young kids couldn't raise money and build a successful business in this environment. My visceral response was, *I'm going to show you I can do this*!

"His feedback reinforced my passion for FashionPlaytes. However, I knew that to make this work, I needed to be confident that I could balance these two critical aspects of my life—work and family life."

At the same time, Sarah also wanted to create a business that would be a role model of empowerment and opportunity for her children. When she consciously weighed the balance of time commitment versus the opportunity of having her children see her creating something out of nothing, she found her solution. "The way I was going to handle that conflict was to make sure my kids were involved in the business," she says.

Today, while Sarah juggles a busy home and growing business, her daughters play a critical role in the direction of her product development. She enjoys fostering a family-business mentality in which everyone feels they can contribute.

Sarah's story is just one of the many we have collected over the years about what makes women entrepreneurs successful. Like Ce Ce, Janice, and Sarah, you may have many great ideas brewing that excite and inspire you.

We want to help you take your ViBI and begin to use your inherent capabilities to shape that into the business you'd like to own. To ensure your success, we'll also help you develop skills in *scanning*—analyzing and understanding how your business fits into the world—*focusing* on the unique aspect of your business, and *thriving* in your business and life.

Your Role in the SmartGirls Way

This book focuses on steps and connections for taking your vision and making it a reality. We provide you with an understanding of your strengths and the methodology to identify and leverage them; your role is to do the work.

The most important outcome from these tools is to use the outputs to inform, aid, and strengthen your community of **champions**: friends, financiers, suppliers, business partners, supporters, and others who will follow your progress, get the word out about you and your business, and, most important, become your future customers.

One of the things that you and only you can determine is how your ViBI fits into your life. Understanding your values from the beginning will make it easier to keep your life and business in balance. The important thing to understand about balance is that it is a fluid state that shifts from day to day as your business shifts and morphs. Balance is not about keeping both sides of a scale equally aligned at all times, but rather about making sure the scale doesn't tip too far in one direction for too long. Here are a few critical steps to consider:

› Have you articulated your personal values to yourself?
› Is your vision for your business aligned with your personal values?
› Do you feel a strong personal connection to your vision?
› Do you wake up and feel good about what you are doing?

A "no" response to any of these questions will tell you where you should focus and reflect. A "yes" response to all four questions indicates you are ready to move forward.

Now that you've begun to define your ViBI, it's time to test it against your SmartGirls Strengths.

Taking the Diagnostic

Before going any further, we recommend that you use the SmartGirls Mirror. This diagnostic is designed to help you understand how your strengths are working for you and your vision, start-up, or business, and how to leverage your strengths to remain aligned, energized, and committed as your business grows.

**To access the tool, go to
http://SmartGirlsWay.com/smartgirls-mirror**

Once you are there, follow the prompts to register for your user ID and password for the diagnostic. When you complete the registration, you will be asked a security question, the answer to which can be found using this copy of the book. For instance, the question might be, "What is the first word on page 27 of your copy of *The SmartGirls Way*?" In that case, the answer would be *your*. When you answer this question, you will receive free access to the test.

Because the diagnostic measures characteristic behaviors against your ViBI, your scores can change as your business grows and evolves. The first step of the diagnostic is to clearly define what stage of entrepreneurship you are in. It is not necessary to be in any particular stage, but how you effectively leverage your SmartGirls characteristics will vary depending upon what stage you are in.

Stage 1: I have a dream or a big idea that I am considering turning into a business.

Stage 2: I am starting a new business.

Stage 3: I want to scale/grow my business.

You can take the diagnostic at any stage of your business. Your code, user ID, and password allow you to take the diagnostic up to three times.

The diagnostic will take you through a series of questions, which will take approximately fifteen minutes.

When taking the diagnostic, think about each question as it relates to your personal experience and where you are *right now* in the development of your ViBI for your business. Answer each question honestly—there are no right or wrong answers.

Once you have answered all of the questions, you will receive your SmartGirls Mirror reflecting your three highest strengths. How you leverage these characteristics and use them to amplify other strengths is the subject of Chapter 4.

4

Interpreting the SmartGirls Mirror

At the SmartGirls Way, we believe in building from strength to strength, and the SmartGirls Mirror is designed to tell you which of the six characteristics of women entrepreneurs are most consistent for you in your business *right now* and how to leverage your strongest characteristics to amplify and optimize others as your business grows.

Before proceeding, please complete the SmartGirls Way diagnostic at http://SmartGirlsWay.com/smartgirls-mirror
(for instructions on how to access the diagnostic
for free, please refer to page 28)

As discussed at the end of Chapter 3, the very first step of the diagnostic is to clearly define what stage of entrepreneurship you are in. How you effectively leverage your SmartGirls Mirror will vary depending upon the stage of your Vision-inspired Big Idea (ViBI).

It is also important to make the distinction between the SmartGirls Mirror characteristics and personality. We all possess Integrity, Creativity, Intuition, Passion, Curiosity, and Weaving skills to some degree. It is not our intention to analyze your personality or determine whether you are a "creative" or "intuitive" person. Instead, the Mirror measures *how* you are using these characteristics in your current situation and reflects where you can leverage these behavior preferences as strengths to fuel other behaviors.

For example, in the diagnostic, when we ask you to respond to the statement "I can easily 'shut off' my creative thinking to execute my ideas," we're not measuring your creativity, we are assessing how well you are **optimizing** it. By *optimize*, we mean how well you are consciously and continuously using this characteristic as a day-to-day strength.

We named our strengths diagnostic the SmartGirls Mirror because we want you to embrace and love what you see. The more honest and reflective you are with yourself, the more you will get out of the tool. And while you may consider yourself a "curious" or "intuitive" person, depending on what is going on within your business, you may find you are leveraging hidden strengths you were unaware of.

If you are surprised by the results of your personalized mirror, don't be discouraged; what is reflected there can help you find blind spots in your commitment and insights into behaviors that may be holding you back. It is critical that you not feel inadequate or try to "fix" a perceived weakness. Instead, look at your top strength scores. What about this strength is working for you, and how can you build on that characteristic for success? (See the optimization table on page 60.)

Interpreting Your SmartGirls Mirror

Once you complete the diagnostic, you will receive a reflection of all six characteristics. Each of the six SmartGirls Way characteristics is represented by a number out of 100, and your top two characteristics will be highlighted for you.

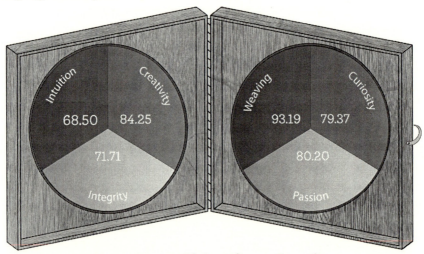

Your SmartGirls Mirror Results

Generally, a score of 80 or higher indicates you are leveraging a characteristic to optimal effect. You will want to look at how these strengths can optimize other behaviors in the table on page 60.

If you receive a score of 60 or below on a characteristic, you may want to look at the ways in which each strength influences others as well as the specific Mirror questions highlighted within each characteristic of this chapter to identify places of conflict, uncertainty about an element of your business, or new opportunities and behaviors that may help you move your business forward.

Internal Strengths

We call Integrity, Intuition, and Creativity the **internal strengths**, as they are typically a reflection of what goes on within you and play a critical role in assessing your desire to invest effort, money, intelligence, time, and other resources that turn your idea or vision into a business.

Specifically, a high Integrity score reveals that you not only are sure of the value of your business idea, but also experience a sense of peace and contentedness with how your ViBI fits within your life. Indicators of this are a true sense of commitment to your core values and pride in the role your business will play in the world.

A high Intuition score indicates that you recognize people and opportunities that are bringing important aspects to your business. You have a sense of what matters and what does not, and you recognize synergies that may not be immediately evident to others.

A high Creativity score indicates you are able to explore opportunities, overcome obstacles, and create important connections to your business idea. The energy, enthusiasm, and sheer number of "sparks" you take away from interactions with others about your idea or business is one way to assess if you're maximizing your creativity.

External Strengths

Once you understand the relative internal strengths of your Mirror, you can begin to mobilize what we refer to as the **external** or **optimizer strengths**. These strengths—Passion, Curiosity, and Weaving—tend to be more visible to the external world. They become strengths when they are balanced and *always working for you.*

Your external strengths tend to be less of a reflection of how you feel about your vision and more a measure of your general competence, preference, and comfort in how you bring that vision to life. From your external-strengths score, you gain a much better understanding of how well you are implementing your ViBI in the world. External strengths are very interdependent upon your internal strengths.

For example, Passion is an incredible energy source—it's a true rocket booster and generally the most common strength of all women entrepreneurs. When your Passion score is very high, it will come across in all aspects of your business. However, Passion can also override your social sensitivity, and may leave people feeling bowled over or overpowered by you. You will need appropriate strategies in order to leverage your Passion to gain the support of others, such as leveraging your Intuition and Creativity to connect your Passion to the ideas of others and convey your Passion in a way that helps you build a supportive network (also a key aspect of Weaving).

When your Curiosity score is very high, you are constantly seeing new opportunities to link ideas and the people you meet in ways that enhance and grow your business. Curiosity can also really spark your Creativity. However, you may also have a tendency to become distracted or head down paths that are not productive. To balance this, you will need to use your Intuition and Integrity as barometers for your actions.

When your Weaving score is very high, it may seem that everywhere you turn, you manifest connections with people, places, and ideas that directly benefit your business. Conversely, if your score is low, it may be because you need to take a step away from your business in order to identify patterns and linkages. Or perhaps you are ignoring your Intuition or need to take a closer look at your Integrity score.

Your SmartGirls Mirror profile will help you identify your natural strengths, as well as signal potential blind spots. In the following pages, we outline how each characteristic can work for you—and against you—when formulating, launching, and managing your business.

The SmartGirls Mirror Characteristics

Integrity

Integrity is defined as the honest and unimpaired adherence to our moral principles.[1] We each have our own unique set of personal beliefs that define who we are. In the context of the SmartGirls Way, Integrity is the strength that addresses the impact and actions of your business and the treatment of others that is characterized by justice, fairness, and impartiality. For the majority of women we interviewed for this book, a sense of Integrity was a critical catalyst for starting their businesses. When making critical decisions about her business, a woman is more likely to consider the long-term impact of those decisions. We see this play out in the incredibly high rate at which women repay their loans and in the rate at which women-owned businesses give back to charities and communities.[2, 3]

When it comes to launching and growing a business, if we do not build businesses that are aligned with our personal Integrity, we have a very hard time making the necessary commitments that allow our business to succeed.

The SmartGirls Mirror can help you test the Integrity of your ViBI by looking at how consistently your actions, expectations, and outcomes are aligned with your personal values and beliefs.

The SmartGirls Way Perspective One of the biggest differences between men and women is how we verbally respond to a business issue that triggers our Integrity. A woman will explain her Integrity conflict using feeling words: "This just doesn't feel right to me." The feelings statement often opens the door for others to dissuade and distract us from our resolve. A man, however, may be more decisive in his reaction and effectively draws a line in the sand, saying, "This is against my principles."

One way you can better convey and manage Integrity challenges you may experience in your business is to pay attention to how you talk about those conflicts. Being clear, direct, and open will often suit you better than a passive or emotional approach.

Studies have also shown that as a gender, we tend to be more overt and aware of the motivations behind our Integrity, and this certainly plays out in the reasons that women start down an entrepreneurial path in the first place.[4] Women are less willing to make the trade-offs between making a difference and making money. We believe that women can make a difference *and* make money, and the secret to this is to start a business that addresses a specific, and sometimes very personal, need.

Integrity in Action

For Amra Tareen, Integrity was the catalyst for her to create AllVoices.com. As a Muslim and the mother of two boys growing up in San Francisco after 9/11, she was frustrated by the editorial bias that was coming across in much of the news coverage on the Middle East. So she decided to do something about it.

She designed a Web platform that invites citizens from all over the world to report on what they are observing in their local areas. These on-the-ground snapshots gave voice to everyday views of events and experiences without the filter and editorial bias of news outlets or governments. Journalists, who could report directly from their location, also fed information to AllVoices.

As the site grew, Amra's Integrity continued to drive the principles behind the content: "My prior background in technology and venture capital had taught me to value economies of scale. I knew that if I was going to scale to the high-volume targets in my business plan, I needed to create a platform that wasn't just dedicated to a political agenda but would represent everyone's need for all kinds of news and topics without an unfiltered bias."

Today, AllVoices.com is the largest citizen-journalists/global news site and as of January 2011 receives 11 million unique visitors each month. *Read more about Amra's story in Chapter 9.*

For women, Integrity can often overlap with Intuition because of our highly refined sense of communication and social sensitivity skills. We readily recognize when people aren't connecting or working in an integral way. For many women, these intuitive interactions trigger something in our sense of Integrity and can become a catalyst for making a big change—they may even be the driving force that starts us down an entrepreneurial path. ViBIs are often sparked by a need we see that resonates with our personal values. And this is a common thread in the SmartGirls Way Integrity score.

Integrity is the directional compass of your business.

When a women entrepreneur is working from a high sense of Integrity, she has a clear sense of direction.

Integrity helps us to find "true north" and stay on course. When a woman entrepreneur is working from a high sense of Integrity, she wakes up feeling excited and eager about her day. She finds it easy to explain her business to others because she can readily find hooks and angles that help others become aligned and connected to it.

A high sense of Integrity allows her to navigate around issues and obstacles without getting off track, losing her enthusiasm, or getting distracted.

Because she is being genuine with herself, she is fueled by her beliefs and can objectively evaluate the positive and negative implications of her business on her personal life, her community, and society as a whole. And when her business is aligned with her personal Integrity, she is more likely to find those creative solutions to build supportive networks and systems that allow her to continue with her venture.

Conversely, when something (or someone) in her business goes against her Integrity, she may lose all enthusiasm for that person or the business.

When a women entrepreneur is working from a high sense of Integrity, her vision for her business and her life are in balance.

One of the areas in which women often experience Integrity conflicts is when her business and family life are not aligned. Let's face it: There are times when we have to make difficult choices, and the impact of those choices often involves a trade-off. Any woman who has had to balance the impact of business on her personal life (e.g., as a mother or caregiver) is all too familiar with the idea of compromise and sacrifice. If you've had honest conversations with yourself, you know going into your business that there will be times when you have to make trade-offs. If your business is underscored by your sense of Integrity, you may be more satisfied with the trade-offs you have to make in your personal life and feel a greater sense of wholeness with how your business fits with your lifestyle.

> ### Leveraging Your Integrity
>
> When looking at your Integrity score, ask yourself the following questions:
>
> Does my business fit with this understanding?
>
> Have I been radically honest with myself and others about what is required for success?
>
> Does my understanding of my values come across in my conversation with all of my stakeholders?
>
> When something or someone goes against my ideas, do I lose enthusiasm for my business, or does it propel me ahead?
>
> Are the trade-offs I have to make to launch this venture acceptable to me and my personal life?
>
> Was I initially over-the-top excited about this venture but now can't seem to make it happen?
>
> Do I understand my personal values, what I stand for, and what I believe?

Integrity is a strength when you derive a sense of excitement, pride, and wholeness from your business and its impact on others. It becomes easier to explain your business to others. You can find common ground on which to communicate, and you more readily find hooks and angles to communicate to your customers, suppliers, and investors with passion and conviction.

Here's how you can tell if you are maximizing your Integrity as a strength:

	When It's Working for You	When It's Not Working
Integrity	• You are feeling good about how your business will fit into your life.	• You are conflicted or unsure about how your business will fit into your life.

	When It's Working for You	When It's Not Working
Integrity	• You can connect your business purpose to your life purpose. • You can visualize yourself living this life and feeling excited about all that goes with your business. • You are extremely proud to tell the story of your business. • You can articulate how your business fits in the community and the essential and unique characteristics that make it THRIVE. • You understand the impact that your business makes on the world, not only in terms of profit but also on the people you employ and serve, and the community you live and operate within.	• You have not been able to communicate to your loved ones the commitments you will need to make your business succeed. • You have not clarified for yourself how the diverse elements of your life will fit together. • You are overcompensating for your desire to have a business by overprotecting and overproviding in other areas of your life. • You are apologetic for your dream. • You talk about your business idea and dreams only to strangers. • You are unsure of how your business may impact the broader community.

Intuition

We've all heard the phrase *woman's intuition*. It is a saying that came into being in the 1950s to explain how a woman would just *know* things about her husband or children without having to ask. In reality, women *do* have a very high social sensitivity when it comes to many aspects of unspoken communication. For centuries, we've relied on our instincts to make the best decisions for ourselves and others, and we've learned to pay attention to our instincts when something "just isn't quite right."

Today, the more scientific explanation of **Intuition** is the *adaptive unconscious*. This is the mental process that works rapidly and automatically—from relatively little information—to come to a conclusion or make decisions. In his book *Blink,* Malcolm Gladwell calls this "thin-slicing": the ability to gauge what is really important from a very narrow period of experience.[5]

Everyone has Intuition at some level. The **Myers-Briggs Type Indicator (MBTI)** personality test has dedicated an entire trait and subtype to how people use their Intuition when relating to the outside world. Intuition is often hailed as a strength when it helps us to make expert judgments in the blink of an eye, yet it can also be detrimental when it triggers emotional responses and stereotypes that cloud our objectivity with emotion.

The SmartGirls Way Perspective We are just beginning to understand the way the human mind processes and stores information, but one thing is clear: Women are more often thought to be more concerned about (if not more aware of) people's perceptions and feelings, and are subconsciously gathering vast amounts of unspoken information through noting facial expressions and body language.[6] Historically, a woman's Intuition about how something is going to be accepted can be invaluable.

In an entrepreneurial context, we have often seen problems arise in the different ways in which men and women articulate their responses to the intuitive hits we get about a person, setting, or situation. A man may say: "I'm getting the sense that . . .," while a woman will describe that same sense with a feeling word: "This is feeling really . . ."

And feelings in the business world are often ignored.

Intuition is the internal thermostat of our business.

For women to consistently leverage Intuition as a strength in business, we must learn to recognize the difference between an intuitive "hit" and an emotional response, which women often override or ignore.

When a woman follows her Intuition, she pays attention to body memory and external signals.

In a business context, your Intuition may guide you to make decisions about the timing of your business launch, the location of your storefront, or the suppliers you choose to partner with because "it just feels right." Intuition can also guide you in your intrapersonal interactions with potential partners, customers, or investors. The emotional indicator is that

> **Intuition in Action**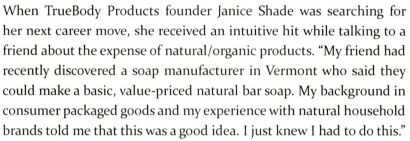
>
> When TrueBody Products founder Janice Shade was searching for her next career move, she received an intuitive hit while talking to a friend about the expense of natural/organic products. "My friend had recently discovered a soap manufacturer in Vermont who said they could make a basic, value-priced natural bar soap. My background in consumer packaged goods and my experience with natural household brands told me that this was a good idea. I just knew I had to do this."
>
> Janice wrote up a business plan and started investigating how she was going to build the company. When her friend decided he needed to focus on other opportunities, her Intuition told her not to give up, so she bought him out of his share of the concept and took on the idea herself. Today, TrueBody's soap is sold on both coasts of the United States. For Janice, Intuition continues to be her driving strength: "I try to make time every day to listen to my Intuition. I walk in the woods or set aside time to just reflect and listen to the cues inside of me." *You can read more about Janice and her story in Chapter 9.*

you feel threatened and defensive. The intuitive "hit" is that this person may not be acting in your best interest or has motives that are not clear or up-front.

When Intuition sparks a strong physiological response, you may read it as emotion and tend to ignore it. When it's bad, it can manifest itself in nausea, vulnerability, or anxiety. In these situations, you may not be clear about (or even aware of) the nature of a problem, but your Intuition can serve as an internal alarm that should make you stop and pay attention to the external signals around you. Instead of reacting emotionally, taking a step back and exploring the reasons behind an intuitive hit (both positive and negative) can be very enlightening and empowering. Doing something with that data is even more critical.

A woman entrepreneur can leverage Intuition as part of her decision-making process.

Women starting out in business are constantly receiving advice (solicited or not) from people we know and encounter. Often, that advice may contradict what we know internally to be true. When you encounter feedback that goes against your Intuition, it is helpful to pause and examine the facts. However, relying on just the facts alone can also be misleading; sometimes, there is more to the picture than just what's on paper.

Intuition is most useful when you treat it as useful data to help you understand what you are sensing, seeing, or feeling and use it to interpret and extrapolate relevant meaning to any given problem set. Intuition allows you to pull in forms of knowledge you don't necessarily even know you have and establish the importance and priority of different pieces of *hard* and *soft* data.

Using Intuition effectively means intentionally turning it toward a particular problem, idea, or situation.

> **Leveraging Your Intuition**
>
> When looking at your Intuition score, ask yourself the following questions:
>
> What is it about this opportunity that is making me excited?
>
> What is my gut telling me about this market, this competitor, this environment?
>
> Why did I experience such a strong reaction? What was it that made this person stand out to me?
>
> If I were to look at my role in this situation from another person's perspective, what would he or she perceive is making me uncomfortable?
>
> Why am I not feeling more confident about my idea or proposal?
>
> What does this person need from me?

From a SmartGirls Way perspective, our Intuition helps us take in the slices of information we receive and relate them to a person, information, or situation. One of the slices of information we get is emotional, and our emotions are there to tell us something. You need to give Intuition its due. Knowing the difference between an intuitive response and an emotional response is a critical SmartGirls Way skill. Here's how you can test how your Intuition is working:

	When It's Working for You	**When It's Not Working**
Intuition	• It's guiding you toward people and ideas with potential. • You are getting strong positive hits. • You are finding people who can bring something to your vision. • You are finding people who can give you feedback that saves you time and money. • You are following ideas that lead to breakthrough or "scaling" moments. • You are feeling more confident about your intuition. • Your body tells you it was good, and you feel positive; others can hear it in your voice; your significant others would say you were "up." • The fire in your belly is excited and scared.	• You are feeling flat or not getting a vibe about your idea or the meeting. • You are becoming resistant to the feedback you are getting from the people you are seeking. • You are meeting with people who make you uncomfortable. • You are taking input that changes the essence of your vision. • You feel your basic integrity or values are being compromised. • You are not energized and are not remaining optimistic. • The fire in your belly is just scared.

Creativity

All human beings are born creative. It is part of the magic of our brain evolution. **Creativity** has been the catalyst behind many successful entrepreneurs from Richard Branson to J. K. Rowling, who dared to wonder, *what if?*

Whether you're launching a business or grappling with a major obstacle, one of the best gifts you can give yourself is to unleash your Creativity. When we explore the outer limits of our ideas, we create a visual picture of how our business will look when it is thriving, and also uncover solutions, opportunities, and breakthroughs on the path to success.

When you focus and harness this Creativity, you begin to visualize your dreams not only for yourself, but for the other partners, investors, stakeholders, and customers you take along on that journey.

The SmartGirls Way Perspective An area of the brain called the *corpus callosum* is where most connections between known and perceived data are made. It serves as the bridge between the creative and feeling centers of the brain and the logical and data-collection/sorting areas of the brain. There are distinct differences in metabolic levels, shape, and function between the female and the male corpus callosum.[7] While studies continue, evidence is building that women are using this part of the brain more effectively as it relates to connecting many modalities and loosely affiliated concepts. This turns out not only to be helpful in Intuition, but also to be a strong aspect of Creativity.

In business, women often have a hard time being direct when asking for what they want; self-confidence—particularly when it comes to raising capital—continues to be an inhibiting factor for women. Women entrepreneurs are more likely to express a fear of failure than our male counterparts.[8] In a culture that tends to encourage the judgment of others, we often see women limiting themselves. Creativity can be the tool that pushes women over that hurdle. Over the years, many women entrepreneurs have told us that their best advice is to *dream big*.

Indeed, many women we've interviewed started their companies because they felt a sense of being creatively unfulfilled, or they saw a more creative solution to an unmet problem.

Creativity is your company's innovation center.

When a woman effectively taps her Creativity,
she gives herself room for focused exploration.

By creating an environment/company culture that allows you to follow new leads and sources of inspiration and encourages others to do the same, you come ever closer to making the connections and gaining the insights that secure your business. When you allow your Creativity to flow without judgment, you explore new avenues, new channels, and new partnerships.

Although studies show that men and women possess equal creative abilities, the ways in which we express and view our Creativity are thought to be different, and there is a distinct correlation between self-confidence and Creativity in women.[9] Research into the differences in Creativity are more definitive in terms of how different kinds of Creativity work—including those more typically produced by women and by men—and are valued by society.

This may explain why the women we talk to feel they are culturally conditioned to be more comfortable and open with the tactile expression of Creativity as an expression of inner views and ideals. Artists, musicians, sculptors, and especially mothers find ways to facilitate creative expression through tactile exploration and spatial awareness. We see this play out in the ways in which we express ourselves through our dress and decorate our homes. And there is no reason why this same creative touch can't positively impact your business.

Creativity is a critical component of an entrepreneur's DNA and is often synonymous with innovation.[10] In the early days of your venture, you will probably be testing your ideas on friends and family, and constantly exploring and reading about anything and everything to do with your business. One of the attractions—and downfalls—of entrepreneurship for many people is that it can be limitless. In this sense, your Creativity can also be an inhibitor. When the idea-generating entrepreneur responsible for leading a group is constantly changing course, it can distract, demotivate, and derail her team. Knowing when to stop creating and start implementing can be a pivotal and painful moment for the entrepreneur. This is where Intuition and Passion can help focus Creativity. Knowing when to follow an idea that leads you to a new insight must be balanced with the roll-up-your-sleeves dedication that brings your creative dream to fruition. Keeping a journal of ideas and capturing those loose associations and moments of inspiration when they happen is critical. Channeling your Creativity to your ViBI is essential.

A woman can leverage her creativity
to overcome barriers and solve problems.

No matter how sound your business idea, you will encounter challenges and barriers. Women entrepreneurs who leverage Creativity as a strength often do so by finding creative ways to get around obstacles.

> ### Creativity in Action
>
> The story of Gretchen Schauffler, founder of Devine Color, clearly demonstrates the use of Creativity to overcome obstacles.
>
> When her knack for creating customized paint colors for friends and family grew into a custom design business in Oregon, Gretchen never dreamed she'd actually evolve that business into a manufacturing endeavor.
>
> "It took a 6,000-square-foot mistake to make me stop in my tracks. The painter mixed one of my custom colors, but the end result was a dull, greasy finish that actually looked 'sweaty' on the walls. At this point, I understood that if I was going to make custom colors, I actually needed to create the product," she explains.
>
> After a year of searching, Gretchen found Miller Paint, a regional paint manufacturer and retailer who was looking to broaden its appeal to women. The company saw true merit in Gretchen's creative approach, the unique aspects of her design approach, and the composition of her products.
>
> "The paint itself goes on like yogurt; I love creamy, rich yogurt, and I thought that is what the consistency of my paint should be—something that doesn't drip, splatter, or smell, and is delightful to play with," she says.
>
> Today, her Trend-Proof collection boasts a timeless pallet of 128 colors. Her paints' unique textures emulate fabric on the walls and are sold exclusively through the Miller Paint Company. *Read more about Gretchen's story in Chapter 9.*

For an entrepreneur, a primary barrier to Creativity is failing to recognize burnout. When you feel that all your good ideas have been used up, or you are facing a major barrier that could derail your business, it may be time to step away for a time.

Taking a complete break from everything can help you tap into the highly creative state of associative thinking and can consciously spark your unconscious Creativity to emerge in new insights. If you have an idea while driving or taking a shower, take the time to write it down in more than one word.

A change of scenery, a customer focus group, or outside input from a mentor can be just the jump start needed to reenergize your business. You don't need to overcomplicate it, and you don't have to spend a great deal of money. Most likely you already have within your network many creative resources. Host a creative workshop and put those creative resources to work for you. Say you want to start a mobile marketing endeavor to connect parents and teens. You probably know people who have kids between ages ten and thirteen. Invite the women together to brainstorm with you. Join women's networking organizations that encourage open discussions and invite speakers on new trends and topics to participate. Giving yourself time to network and listen to an outside perspective will spark new connections—and then you're off again.

Exploring Your Creativity

You can focus your Creativity by asking yourself:

Do I frequently daydream and allow my mind to freely wonder in new directions?

Do I find myself coming up with many ideas but really get excited about a select few?

Am I energized by people and things around me?

Is there a symbol or mantra that best represents my ViBI?

When faced with a barrier or obstacle, do I stubbornly hold on to my ultimate goal, or do I allow myself to uninhibitedly explore other paths?

Creativity is not the place to limit your thinking or to limit yourself. Here are some ways you can tell if your Creativity is working for you or against you:

	When It's Working for You	When It's Not Working
Creativity	• You are sparking new ideas and opportunities for your ViBI. • Your idea is at the center of a lot of opportunities and connections. • You are creating pictures, graphs, or drawings that help your dream connect. • You are starting to be able to answer creatively questions that people have asked you about your dream. • Your passion has a shape. • You are using many mediums to express yourself. • You can use a medium that you love a lot (words, drawing, expressionist art) to represent your idea (e.g., you can write a poem about your idea). • You can get a little absurd. • You are not self-censoring. • You are feeling limitless and full of potential.	• You feel that all your ideas have already been tried. • You know that you have something to do that is unique and different, but you don't know how to express it. • You feel emotional when you try to do something creative. • You are intimidated by the words and actions associated with creative exercises. • You are worried about involving others in Creativity work with you. • You feel concerned that you are not creative and so you don't start. • You are afraid to be judged.

Passion

When someone is described as "passionate," we get a sense of the power of her feeling. In fact, **Passion** is defined as *an emotion or the visible expression of a strong, barely controllable enthusiasm.*[11] For an entrepreneur,

Passion is fuel. It is the emotion that gives energy, and when used and responded to in tandem with optimizer strengths, it can be the most important **leverage point** for your business.

When you are passionate about your business, you can see the end goal before anyone else does, and it propels you down that path to creating your ViBI, even during the most daunting and challenging of times.

Passion in Action

Heidi Ganahl is founder of Camp Bow Wow, one of the hundred fastest-growing franchises in North America and a leader in the pet-care industry. Like many women entrepreneurs, Heidi's catalyst for her business grew out of an unmet need in an area she was passionate about—animals. When she and her husband couldn't find a boarding solution for their pets, they decided there had to be a better way. Although her business dreams were tabled by the untimely death of her husband, her Passion for animals never waned, and five years later, she picked up the business plan and set out to create the ultimate care environment for pets and their owners. Heidi attributes part of the success of her 111 doggie day and overnight camp locations to the SmartGirls Mirror strength of Passion.

"Passion was what drove me from day one. When you have Passion, it gets you out of bed every morning and keeps you going, even through the tough times," she explains.

Heidi's Passion for animals was also a fundamental component in her success. Her belief that pets should have a healthy, happy, and safe environment when they couldn't be with their owners not only drove every aspect of her business, it revolutionized the doggie day-care industry. *Read more about Heidi's story in Chapter 9.*

The SmartGirls Way Perspective In entrepreneurial ventures, Passion is usually seen as the genesis of the business. This is especially true for women entrepreneurs, for whom feeling successful in life often rests on being able to follow a Passion.[12] It is the incredibly important role of Passion that helps you to find and tap into something you care enough about doing and that keeps you energized through good and bad times alike.

Of all the characteristics, Passion is cited as the most prominent and ever-present strength for women who have taken the SmartGirls Mirror diagnostic.

Passion is often studied in relation to its impact on Creativity. In the field of psychology, entire books have been written about the exuberance and passionate commitment that have fueled great artists, poets, screenwriters, and actors. Many successful entrepreneurs are passionately creative.

However, a challenge arises when the exuberant expression of Passion overcomes reason and common sense. When Passion overrides Intuition, the ability to motivate others is decreased. We become defensive to questions or feedback, ignoring intuitive cues from others because we are not listening.

Passion is rocket fuel for your business engine. Use it wisely.

Passion is such a constant strength among women that we focus here on how to leverage it appropriately in the two most significant roles it plays: the creation and launching of your business.

Passion is the leading edge of the creative process.

The most evident and easy way to access leverage for Passion is the connection between Passion and Creativity. When we become passionate about something, it fuels our creative tendencies, and successful results increase our Passion for the effort.

Passion is the visible evidence to others of your power and commitment.

When talking to women entrepreneurs and the angel investors who back them, we discovered that by and large, women who could credibly and consistently demonstrate Passion toward their ideas displayed the confidence investors needed to move ahead. The conversations that lead to support, endorsement, customers, and success are fueled by Passion.

The ability to energize yourself and others through your desire to see a positive outcome is driven by your Passion. It can be infectious to others when they get a sense of being part of something larger than themselves.

For the woman entrepreneur, Passion manifests itself in the sense that failure is not an option and a sense that your Passion *cannot be denied*. Cultivate, understand, and use your Passion—and you can move your world.

Interpreting the SmartGirls Mirror | 49

> **Exploring Your Passion**
>
> When testing your Passion,
> think about how you would answer the following questions:
>
> When I speak passionately about my business, does it inspire others?
>
> When I speak passionately about my business, do those closest to me support me unconditionally?
>
> When I put my heart and soul into something I believe in, do I succeed?
>
> Will I sincerely regret not following my ViBI?

If your Passion isn't present, it is likely that you haven't really landed on your ViBI. Overamplifying your Passion can also destroy your chances of gaining the support you will need to grow a thriving business. Here are some ways in which you can tell if your Passion is working for you or against you:

	When It's Working for You	When It's Not Working
Passion	• You can articulate your vision in a way that makes others excited and interested in helping. • You get more and more excited the more you learn about the potential for your vision.	• Your ability to communicate your vision is cloudy and overemotional. • You overwhelm people with your enthusiasm for your idea. • You are unable to stop for breath.

	When It's Working for You	When It's Not Working
Passion	• You are not easily discouraged by naysayers or pessimists who give you advice about what you should do. • Thinking and talking about your idea gives you energy and drive to get things done.	• You are not able to listen to other's ideas or are immediately argumentative and defensive. • You can stay positive only if your vision and ideas are on center stage at all times.

Curiosity

In the context of the SmartGirls Way, **Curiosity** is the ability to understand how a particular idea fits in the world. A natural Curiosity will propel us to seek out those ideas that are similar to our own. We are curious about what makes something happen, the "why" of a situation, or the motivations and intentions behind an issue. As women, our Curiosity works as a strength when it focuses us to dig deeper. We also need to understand where our Curiosity should stop. As entrepreneurs, sometimes our Curiosity can get the better of us and lead us down distracting paths.

The SmartGirls Way Perspective One of the most important aspects of managing our Curiosity as entrepreneurs—or managers and most leaders—is to know when it is important to quit thinking or chasing. Women and men are thought to do this differently, and the reason for this lies in the different ways in which women focus.

When comparing women to men, it is believed that men think with "tunnel vision"—using single cues to solve a problem—while women use their minds to synthesize multiple cues from the environment.[13] This ongoing multi-synthesis can be a tremendous attribute when we apply it to our Curiosity, because it may allow us to make a connection or send us down a path of inquiry that a man may tend to ignore in an effort to remain focused on the issue at hand.

Another difference between women and men when it comes to Curiosity can be attributed to social norming. In the past, women were trained to receive and accept information instead of questioning it, challenging it, or wondering about it. A critical inhibitor of Curiosity is a lack of self-confidence. We do ourselves a disservice if we are afraid to ask questions because it exposes what we don't know and forces us to face our fears and uncertainties or to rethink our assumptions.

Curiosity is your research department.

When a woman employs Curiosity, she creates synergies that infuse her business with insights.

You know that you are tapping into your Curiosity when you find yourself searching for answers and learning something new. Nearly every entrepreneur is being exposed to new skill sets and challenges, and Curiosity enables us to follow non-obvious threads to new breakthroughs or recognize when something should be explored in more depth.

When your Curiosity is operating at an optimum level, you have an enthusiasm for learning everything you can about your business. Curiosity will lead you to mentors and others who may know more than you do on a subject, and by having an inquisitive approach to your business, you may find solutions you didn't even know you were seeking.

Curiosity in Action

Ce Ce Chin always knew she wanted to be a designer, but it was curiosity that compelled her to design her first line of footwear. She was trained as a handbag designer but wanted a new creative challenge. She loved shoes, and she began observing what the women of New York City were wearing on their feet: "New York is a walking city, and it contained a life that I understood. I was curious about what shoes typical New York women were wearing, and how the shoes fit into their lives."

Furthermore, in her business planning research, she came upon the **80/20 Principle**, which simply states that approximately 80 percent of the effects come from 20 percent of the causes. Or, 80 percent of the impact comes from 20 percent of the efforts. Coincidentally, she observed how the 80/20 Principle also applied to how women dress and how they favor certain items: "I started noticing what shoes were being worn time and time again, and it reminded me of the old 80/20 adage. In this case, I noticed people wear 20 percent of their shoes 80 percent of the time."

> She concluded that women feel as strongly about what shoes they put on their feet as men feel about what kind of cars they drive—it's an extension of a lifestyle, and literally the shoes are their vehicles for transport.
>
> "I wanted my shoes to be fun-loving, easy, and effortless to wear anywhere—the shoe that people wore 80 percent of the time."
>
> This principle became the basis of her 80%20 brand.
>
> "The collection initially started as a sneaker line. I loved the comfort of sneakers, but they were just, well…flat. I'm five-foot-four, and I wanted to appear taller, but heels weren't really my game. So the hidden wedge grew out of my own need. It's like the padded bra of footwear!"
>
> Six years later, 80%20 Shoes is known for its hidden-wedge shoe design, and has developed a loyal, almost cultlike following. *You can read more about Ce Ce's story in Chapter 9.*

*When a woman leverages her curiosity,
she focuses on learning in a meaningful way!*

When you optimize your Curiosity, you not only are able to design good questions that lead you to effective answers, but also have the ability to understand what is core or central to your learning and what is interesting, but not important. A critical requirement of an entrepreneur during the start-up and scaling of her business is focus. Often, this is counterintuitive to Curiosity when you're excited and exploring everything to do with your industry and market. The ability to recognize when you may be approaching "analysis paralysis" or chasing a diversion that will not add critical value to what you need to know is just as important as allowing yourself to be curious in the first place.

Interpreting the SmartGirls Mirror | 53

> **Exploring Your Curiosity**
>
> When using your Curiosity,
> how would you answer the following questions?
>
> When seeking answers or information, do I look beyond what is obvious?
>
> If something doesn't make sense to me, do I try to find out why?
>
> What am I learning from this conversation, experience, or meeting?
>
> When I face something new or unfamiliar, is there someone I know who can guide me or teach me about this subject?
>
> Is my Curiosity helping me map meaningful connections, or is it leading me off track?

Curiosity is a fantastically powerful tool if you use it to make connections that really work for business and then have the confidence to act on them.

Here are some ways you can tell if you are optimizing your Curiosity:

	When It's Working for You	When It's Not Working
Curiosity	• You have a sense of where to look for information you need to be successful. • You can form questions about what you need to know. • You know when "enough is enough."	• You are intrigued by everything. • You feel more confused and less informed the more you find out. • Your ability to articulate the meaningful questions is decreasing.

Curiosity	When It's Working for You	When It's Not Working
	• You are not distracted into other areas of interest; or if you are, you are able to acknowledge that you are on a tangent. • You know when a tangent might be a very useful thing. • You are cross-pollinating other useful ideas.	• You are not finding the answers to what you seek. • You are easily distracted by interesting but not relevant information, and do not know that you are offtrack. • You lose interest in other ideas and disciplines that may have value, and care only about ideas that are yours or support your thesis.

Weaving

Of all the SmartGirls Way characteristics, **Weaving** is the most uniquely feminine—and our personal favorite. Weaving is a collective strength that uses networking, community building, listening, and social sensitivity skills, as well as communication and multitasking abilities. When you watch true weavers making cloth, their hands move very quickly while constantly changing colors in the pattern. This visual is the ideal metaphor for understanding the patterns and threads that entrepreneurs weave together into a business that is useful, textured, and valuable. When you weave effectively, you are building the fabric and foundation that become the safety net for you, your business, and your family.

Strong weavers are first and foremost great networkers; being a part of a networking organization is a common success factor for women entrepreneurs, but Weaving goes well beyond networking alone.[14] Good networkers create connections and thread people together in straight lines. Weavers create a true fabric, connecting multiple threads and connections and combining webs into whole support systems. Weavers can have big networks and are consciously connecting them—not just because it is the right thing to do but because of the ideas and solutions they see.

The SmartGirls Way Perspective Typically, men approach networking with the intention of, "What do I want to get out of this?" They connect with people because it makes good business sense and ultimately may have a payoff. Women, on the other hand, traditionally network more expansively, seeing how people connect to them and where a community exists in the larger scheme of things. It is one reason that women far outnumber men in social-networking circles.[15] Yet because of our love of connecting communities, networking for women can become a distraction, and as entrepreneurs, we need to create both *balance* and *benefit* from the business groups we join. We need to focus our Weaving.

When we are Weaving, we are constantly managing multiple threads simultaneously. Multitasking is another important distinction between women and men entrepreneurs. When it comes to splitting one's focus among many different activities, women are better than men at more accurately and efficiently completing the important tasks.[16] As mentioned earlier, one of the reasons behind the different approaches of each gender is attributed to the corpus callosum—a little part of the brain that handles communication between the two hemispheres. The corpus callosum is biologically larger or more active in women than in men, and this is one theory as to why women can split their focus more efficiently.[17] This is why, even when there is a lot happening around us, we can quickly hone in with clarity on a business problem or make a snap connection to another solution, business connection, or idea. This fast-firing of the corpus callosum gives women the ability to see patterns of connections and visualize constellations of ideas, people, and markets around our business ideas.

Weaving in Action

The success of Stephanie Allen's Dream Dinners meal-assembly company is rooted in the strength of Weaving. After running a successful catering business for more than twelve years and managing her busy family, she had developed a routine of preparing and freezing healthy meals for her family that lasted her an entire month. Perfecting the concept, she began to share her "secret recipes" with her friends, including another working mom, business and financial expert Tina Kuna. After several successful fix-and-freeze gatherings in Stephanie's kitchen with friends, the two women soon realized they had an opportunity to bring the convenience and camaraderie to other women beyond their circle of friends.

> While the root idea for their company was to help busy women prepare healthy, home-cooked meals, the key driver of their concept was where that dinner was initially created. In the Dream Dinners meal-prep kitchen, women were coming together to get something done—in this case, cooking—and enjoying the connections and community they were creating in the process.
>
> As the company scaled, Dream Dinner party nights became a key component of Stephanie and Tina's business model. Women gathered their friends and hosted "meal-prep parties" where they shared their ingredients as well as their company. These parties became the ultimate customer-referral program as more women planned their own events and invited more women to join in.
>
> As the business took off, Stephanie continued to weave together people and concepts to hone and perfect the Dream Dinners concept.
>
> The business soon developed into a franchise opportunity and became the recognized originator of the $300 million meal-assembly industry. *You can read more about Stephanie's story in Chapter 9.*

Strong weavers are good at communicating and listening.

When you are optimizing your Weaving characteristics, you are picking up on the things that nobody else sees. You are actively listening (often amplifying your Intuition) to find nuances in meaning and seeing both directions of a problem. At the same time, you can communicate the distinctions and differentiators for your business and convey your vision in an articulate and well-thought-out manner. Refining what you know happens only through active listening and presence.

Weaving and Intuition are actively linked; if you have a low score in Intuition, you need to be more active with your Weaving, seeking out data that support your views, and finding allies and partners to augment this skill. You can also tap into your Creativity to foster a stronger Weaving ability, such as allowing time at the end of each day to sit and think about the conversations you had that day, or doing simple word-association exercises to identify new patterns or opportunities.

Weaving amplifies Integrity.

Integrity is about being whole, and Weaving is the ability to see the whole. When we are Weaving effectively, we see the end points and the connections and insights that will help us reach our goals. Even when you don't know exactly how to get to that end point, Weaving helps you see it, visualize it, and articulate to others how it should look when it's right.

Weaving is just as much about letting go and being open as it is about holding all the threads of your business in your hand. The business won't line up if you're not holding clearly, subconsciously and consciously, the vision for what you want to achieve. Often, stepping away from your business and the mad pace of the entrepreneur is the best brain recreation for Weaving. Making room for those inspirational moments that come from long, quiet walks or the camaraderie of friends creates synergies and connections that amplify what you are doing.

> **Evaluating Your Ability to Weave**
>
> Here are some questions to consider when Weaving:
>
> Do I see patterns and connections between my personal and professional life?
>
> Do I help others see important patterns and connections?
>
> Am I successfully balancing multiple thoughts and activities?
>
> Is my network yielding useful connections for myself and others?

Weaving allows you to seize the great relationships and communities that will propel your business forward. When you weave your business around your ViBI, you feel energized, confident, and compelled to move forward because you see the benefits of your business on others around you.

	When It's Working for You	When It's Not Working
Weaving	• You are finding or building useful communities. • You are making connections between connections. • You are seeing possibilities for your business. • You are able to discern when a relationship you are building is both interesting and *relevant* rather than one that is just interesting. • You are making seamless connections to and for others and their ideas. • You are building intentional and committed collaborators. • You are gaining and giving value within these communities. • You are putting your communities to work for your dream. • You are serving a valuable role in the dreams of others without diluting or eroding your capacity to fulfill your dream.	• Emotional reactions to your business idea seem like something you should respond/react to. • You are engaging with a number of communities and people but don't know how the information you are getting applies to your business. • You are unsure how the connections that are being made relate to your idea. • You are giving much more than you are receiving from the connections you are making. • You are not creating new partners, innovators, or advocates from your relationship building. • The communities you are engaged in are not helping you refine your vision or improve and prove your concepts. • Your relationships and community building are going well, but they're actually decreasing your capacity and energy to focus on your business.

Integrating Your SmartGirls Mirror

At the beginning of this chapter, we talked about the difference between internal strengths that drive the formation of your ViBI and external strengths that allow you to launch it into the world. No matter what stage your business is in—or what kind of entrepreneur you set out to become—understanding how to leverage together all of the characteristics in the SmartGirls Mirror will help you stay on course.

No single characteristic works alone, and when you are most challenged, you may find many ways in which you can leverage your strongest characteristic to amplify others. For example, Curiosity amplifies your Integrity, and Passion inspires your Creativity. The table on the following pages is an example of the many ways you can draw upon your strengths to amplify other characteristics.

At this point, you should have completed your SmartGirls Mirror and received your score.

To use this table, find your top two strengths in the left-hand column. The highlighted column is the description of that strength. You can scan across and down the table to see how each of your strengths relates to and influences others.

	Integrity	Intuition	Creativity
Integrity	Integrity's prime purpose is alignment. It supports you in the creation of your ViBI and a business that is aligned with your personal values. Integrity also aids you in the development of your personal strengths, ensuring they are consistently applied in the right direction for success.	When your life and business goals are aligned, you can trust your Intuition to guide you to intentionally make sound decisions for your business.	Integrity brings clarity and focus to your Creativity. It is the key to keeping your creative energy flowing and enables you to seek out solutions that will guide you in directions that will help your business.
Intuition	Your Intuition will let you know when you are about to make a decision that is out of alignment with your business goals and personal Integrity. Whether it is a gut feeling or a small nagging voice, if it won't leave you alone, it's your Intuition. Listen!	The primary role of your Intuition is to give you the important information and clues you need to make decisions. To use it effectively, give it the last word when making business decisions. No one ever regrets *not* listening to Intuition.	Intuition and Creativity go hand in hand, especially during the start-up or creation phases of your business. Your Intuition will guide you to avenues of Creativity that your logical, left-brain self would likely not pursue. Tap into Intuition to help your Creativity navigate you through (and around) obstacles.
Creativity	Bringing balance to your life is often the largest hurdle you will face as an entrepreneur. Creativity and Integrity work holistically to help you. What you must do to meet all of the different requirements of your business and your life will not always be apparent. List the needs and then start brainstorming. You'll be amazed what you come up with.	Creativity and Intuition are business-building buddies. While your Intuition guides you in directions worth exploring, your Creativity provides your conscious and unconscious mind with constant feedback and opportunities for exploration. Your Intuition then sorts these opportunities again and focuses (or refocuses) your creative self.	Creativity is both a problem-solver and an energy-booster for your other strengths. If you are running into obstacles or running a little low on energy, you can use Creativity to bring new perspectives and solutions into your business. Creativity is essential for putting the fun back into your ViBI and helps you and your team lighten up when needed.
Passion	Passion strengthens Integrity by providing a critical ingredient—determination. When you are passionate about something, you really need it to happen! Passion ensures you find ways to make your ViBI fit within the context of your life. Passion is your greatest ally in creating a robust, integrated ViBI that you will see to fruition!	Passion is the tuning fork for Intuition, and together, these strengths influence your ViBI like nothing else. We are tuned into the things we are passionate about, and the things we are passionate about rise to the top of our inner radar. Passion gives our Intuition direction.	Passion is the "chocolate treat" that boosts your Creativity. When your Creativity is waning, you can strengthen and refresh by tapping your Passion. Passion is most effective when expressed out loud. If you're finding it difficult to be creative on behalf of your venture, you are probably not talking about it enough. Talk it up. Get others excited. Get your creative self back in the game.
Curiosity	When we apply Curiosity to a loosely held vision or dream, it begins to shape that idea into a genuine intention, ViBI, and business. A well-designed question about an idea that you love plants a seed of intention. Curiosity supplies the needed thrust to begin finding the answers to that question.	Curiosity can serve as Intuition's coach and counselor. It helps you to stay in a questioning mode when your Intuition is already racing to conclusions. It helps you to listen to others, even when your Intuition has told you what to do. *You never know*, it seems to say, *there might be something to learn here. I'm curious.* Let's listen.	Curiosity helps to sharpen Creativity's edge. When you exercise Curiosity's voice, it engages your creative mind on issues that might seem far outside the immediate or relevant. It can also serve to focus your Creativity along the lines that you are most curious about at the moment—a key differentiator if you are linking Curiosity and Intuition.
Weaving	Weaving is the logical starting point for Integrity because it is the beliefs, ideals, and people around you that most inform your Integrity. Weaving helps you keep this community connected and constantly brings you more options for strengthening your vision through networks and ideas that affirm and support your integrated ViBI.	Weaving provides many places where and people with whom you can work and hone your Intuition. By working first in part of your network and with ideas that you can test and validate, you can check your Intuition and get used to listening to that voice. This effort helps when you have many people in your network advising and cajoling, and the inner voice is at risk of being drowned out.	Weaving is the raw-material factory for Creativity. The connections that you make between ideas, people, communities, past experience, and your vision for the future are birthed in your creative mind. The people whom you connect to and weave together comprise the medium for your Creativity, and their creative energy sparks more Creativity in you and in the network around you.

Interpreting the SmartGirls Mirror | 61

	Passion	Curiosity	Weaving
Integrity	Passion is a tremendously beneficial outward-facing strength. It is the key to engaging customers, media, partners, and funders. Rely on your Integrity to keep your Passion directed and specific to your goals.	Integrity is the taskmaster and the guide for your Curiosity. It will help you keep pushing for the answers that will meet the goals of your integrated ViBI. Integrity will also keep you focused on those things that are most critical to your business at any given time.	Integrity partners with Weaving to guide the choices you make, the people you choose to engage with, and the different knowledge, networks, and opportunities you thread together.
Intuition	Passion is one of our most powerful tools, and your Intuition can help you harness it when you're building and talking about your ViBI to others. Passion needs to be engaging and exciting rather than overwhelming. Use the highly developed social sensitivity that is part of your Intuition to make sure you're striking just the right tone for getting others on board with your Vision.	Intuition may send you down paths that might not always make sense to others; but if you listen, it will tell you when you just *know* you need to dig deeper. Go ahead and focus your Curiosity on what you intuitively feel matters and give yourself time to understand what you have learned.	Intuition guides you to the ideas, people, and networks you most need to be successful. Do your research, but let Intuition weigh in regularly as you sort out the "good to know" from the "great to know." Intuition can guide you to hidden networks and relationships that you might not otherwise recognize as unique opportunities for your business.
Creativity	Creativity can be Passion's muse. It can renew your Passion and identify the breakthroughs that keep you headed down the right path. Look for Passion and Creativity to create momentum by constantly reinforcing the direction and importance of your ViBI.	Creativity is Curiosity's implementation arm. As your Curiosity points you in the direction of extremely important questions to answer and opportunities to explore, your Creativity goes to work to see how what you learn applies (or doesn't) to your business. Creativity will uncover the answers for your curious mind.	Creativity informs Weaving by creating connections between people, ideas, and networks that are beyond your normal Weaving patterns. Creativity gives you new ways to connect existing ideas, new reasons to connect with important communities, and new ways to engage key people.
Passion	Passion's primary role as a strength magnifier is to add the energy and fire that comes only from caring about something very deeply. It can bring meaning to your efforts and carry you through when others may give up…that is, until they pick up on your Passion!	Passion strengthens Curiosity by instilling a deep desire to know everything you possibly can about taking your vision forward. It inspires you to go down side roads you might not otherwise explore. When you are passionate about your venture's success, it allows you to take criticism and input from others even when you might not be excited to hear it.	Passion strengthens Weaving by providing the necessary energy for the incredible amount of outreach, networking, connecting, and engaging you will need to succeed. As your business progresses, you can leverage Passion to take your Weaving energy in the direction where your business is headed.
Curiosity	Curiosity serves as an advisor to Passion. The *most* important thing about Passion is that it spreads. Your ability to be curious about what is working, how your Passion is affecting others, and where it is that you can best leverage your passionate expression is a function of being curious about how your Passion is received.	The role of Curiosity is to keep you looking, keep you thinking, and keep you searching. Curiosity as a strength is the most natural antidote to fear, uncertainty, and doubt because it motivates action. Curiosity compels you to keep looking and keep challenging. Curiosity applies action and momentum to all the other strengths.	Curiosity works hand in hand with Weaving by constantly asking, "How are these things connected and interrelated?" Curiosity helps make the most of every opportunity to engage. Curiosity helps leverage relationships through honest interest and an interest in creating win-win-win scenarios in all of your interactions.
Weaving	Weaving provides the people, places, and networks where you can express your Passion. You leverage it to find the talent, investors, advisors, and customers critical to your success. Weaving supports you in knitting these new champions into the fabric of your support structure and create increasingly powerful connections within (and between) these communities.	Weaving facilitates the robust thinking that feeds and directs your Curiosity. When you weave, you make many connections about information you already know, allowing you to target your research. Effective weavers save themselves a lot of time because they have already thought through many connection possibilities, but they still allow themselves to be curious about how they leverage those connections.	Weaving's primary role is to see opportunities within separate threads and strengths to create cohesive ideas and connections within—and beyond—your business. When you understand the power of weaving for others as well as for your business, you benefit from the diversity and idea infusion into your business and life.

Understanding your **SmartGirls** Mirror is the foundation for bringing your ViBI to life. Leveraging these characteristics as strengths can help you develop the business skills, attitude, and confidence to build your business plan, launch your business, and scale and grow it into a thriving enterprise.

5

SCAN

Entrepreneurship typically takes a little more gumption, a little more self-confidence and belief in your idea, and a little more discipline than traditional business management. We want women entrepreneurs to know that there is a process that can help manage the challenges, risks, and worries that come with being an entrepreneur. We call this the **SmartGirls Way Methodology**, and it breaks the process down into three distinct phases that put you on the path to growing your ViBI.

The SmartGirls Way Methodology is designed to provide a more practical and stepwise approach to entrepreneurship in a context that typically doesn't happen in an entrepreneurial venture. Think of this process as planting a seed and then tending it as it grows and blooms. By hitting the milestones within each phase, you will have what you need to create your business plan, launch your venture, and grow and scale your business in a way that stays true to your vision.

Exploring, creating, and launching your ViBI doesn't have to be onerous, and in the early stages, the Methodology will help you bring clarity to your idea. Following these steps will help you identify how much work you have to put into this venture and avoid wasting resources and time later on. Different stages of the process will draw upon different SmartGirls Way characteristics, tools, and exercises, so look for the SmartGirls Mirror boxes that indicate strengths you can leverage for each step.

The first step in the SmartGirls Way Methodology is SCAN.

SCAN stands for **S**ee, **C**onnect, **A**nalyze, and **N**est.

When you SCAN, we want you to do so in a really thoughtful way—to be open versus closed.

The SmartGirls Way SCAN process will help you gain perspective on your ViBI. As you SCAN, you're getting a bird's-eye view, and from this broader context, you can begin to see where movement and payoff are likely to happen.

The SCAN phase is the research and planning phase that will help you build your business plan in an informed way. It is about measuring the context and community where your customer and your ViBI reside. SCAN combines the market-research element of your business plan with the freedom to brainstorm and the discipline to stay focused on your objective.

It's important that you keep your Passion engaged throughout the process, because when you start to SCAN, you will encounter competitors and other barriers. This is the point at which many budding entrepreneurs become discouraged and stop. But if you stick with the process and rely on your SmartGirls Mirror and the tools included in the book, you can see it through and, more important, find out what you need to know to make informed decisions about your business. In the end, you may come up with a creative way to bring your business to market that will not only differentiate you but also help your business to create a positive impact on your family, community, and economy.

See

SCANning effectively begins with clearly seeing the opportunity, competition, business climate, and challenges. Whether you do direct market research or just put out feelers, this step requires that you go beyond your existing network to get the background to design a viable business.

This is the best kind of action research. By acting on it, you move from thinking about your ViBI to finding a way for it to fit into the world.

Start by asking two questions:

› Who are your customers?

> Who are your competitors?

1. Who are your customers?

What do your customers look like? What are their social and demographic behaviors? Where do they reside, and what influences them? Can you break them down into specific groups?

The best way to get a profile of your customers is to get out and talk to some of them. Here are some questions to consider when doing this:

> What benefit will you provide your customers?
> What are the access points to reach them?
> What is the overall size of your market?

The answers can help you create a picture of your customer in your mind that you can connect with.

In middle of 2009, Jane Hoffer was building her second technology company, a gaming platform centered on children aged six to twelve years. "We were going through our prototype for our technology and looking at where our primary target market was aggregating as well as online gaming populations in general," she says. "This was right around the time that Facebook was really taking off, and we discovered that the largest population growth (by percentage, not actual number) on Facebook that fall was women fifty-five and older. We also noticed that the most heavily trafficked site on the American Association of Retired Persons website was their online gaming page. This data began to support a hypothesis that the aging boomer generation was becoming more technology-savvy and was rapidly adopting social-media platforms to connect with their families."

This research into the specific profile of her target customer shifted her strategy to a new direction. "We literally stopped our development to make sure we could change the center of the platform archetype from the child online to the family online and leverage a social demographic that was by nature already coming together," she explains.

The following is an example of how Jane profiled her target customer for Ohanarama.com.

Creating a Customer Profile
Jane Hoffer, Ohanarama.com

Kids	Parents	Grandparents	Disconnected Verticals
Kids aged 6-12 who enjoy gaming. Within this, our sweet spot is kids 6-9. Technology is part of their DNA.	Their parents, who are increasingly concerned about the time their children spend online and the quality and safety of that time. Middle- and upper-class.	Their grandparents, 50% of whom in the U.S. live more than 200 miles away from their children. Boomers are becoming technology-savvy and looking for innovation and meaningful engagements with their grandchildren. They have time and money and seek social interaction Increasingly driven toward brain games.	Other family situations that require being away from one another for long periods of time. Military families. Traveling parents (road warriors). Immigrant/expat families (Asian families in particular) who have come to the U.S. to work and have left behind family members.

To complete the exercises in this chapter as well as more exercises to help you develop your ViBI, visit SmartGirlsWay.com to purchase the *SmartGirls Way Workbook*.

2. Who are your competitors?

Go out and look at what similar businesses offer. What have been their challenges? How would your business be different? What customer needs are not being met?

You decide the criteria by which you want to measure your competitors, but capture these criteria in a way that allows you to visually compare your business to your competitors.

Jane Hoffer looked at both true competitors like Togetherville, an online gaming site launched in May 2010 that had recently been acquired by Disney, and other activities that would compete with the free time families had to play games.

"You have to look at a very high level at the free-time element. In the case of Ohanarama, we knew that a child still likes to play with other toys and activities, and that parents are concerned about monitoring 'screen time,'" explains Jane. "So we specifically designed our games to be ten-minute segments so that they didn't interfere with busy schedules and could still bring families together in a meaningful way."

The following is how Jane filled in her **competitive matrix**.

Building Your Competitive Matrix

Jane Hoffer, Ohanarama.com

	Togetherville	Free time
Criteria to measure them by:	Targeted at young children	Other social and free-time activities
What are the goods and services produced?	Online gaming platform for young children with a social-media integration aspect	Other children, toys, activities, family time, television
What are their core brands, features, and services?	Parents are central to approving this kid-centric platform.	We will need to fit into the busy lives of our target audience. Competing with entertainment, educational and brain time.
What is their path to market?	It became evident that Togetherville was a safe training world for future Facebook and social-networking members, and parental control was their primary focus.	We will need to be sensitive to time commitment, attention span, and concerns about too much screen time. Our platform should focus on short (ten-minute) engagements that focus more on the interaction than the learning of a new game.

Size Your Market

Next, you will need to determine the overall size of your market. How much of this total market do these competitors hold? Much of this information is available online, but if you can't find it, seek out experts in the field and talk to them. One of the most important statistics you can have is the market potential for your business.

When Jane set out to build and fund Ohanarama, she had to capture the potential market for gaming against other online activities for kids. While there was an international potential for her solution, she looked at the domestic market first.

"The insight here was that there was a 'guilt' issue with grandparents because they are not close by and can't be there to spend time with their grandkids," Jane says. "We felt we could capture a small percentage of the social transactions associated for this demographic to be successful."

Sizing Your Market
Jane Hoffer, Ohanarama.com

Kids	Parents	Grandparents
There are 24 million children in the U.S. aged 6-12.	Parents are spending $5 billion a year on games and educational supplements.	Grandparents spend $50 billion annually on their grandkids for vacations, clothing, toys, etc.

Path to Market

Your path to market includes your supply chain (where you will get your materials or intellectual property for delivering your product or service), your distribution (how you will get your product out into the market), and customer access (how you will access your customers). Understanding your path to market is essential in determining how much to invest in creation and delivery of your product so that you can determine later on if the effort and investment are worth it.

Defining Your Path to Market

Jane Hoffer, Ohanarama.com

How will you source/manufacture your product?	We needed to get to market on a very low budget. We realized we didn't have to make everything, so we focused on creating a technology platform that could plug into existing content. To accelerate our time to market, many of our games are licensed games that have been modified to our platform, such as checkers and memory games.
	We then focused our own talent on creating content that didn't already exist in the market and focused on the social interaction between our audience, such as our family quiz game, "Relativity," where family members ask and answer questions about one another.
How will you deliver your product to your customers? (Do you need a distributor? Will you sell it online?)	We knew there was an aggregation of family members who were already connected on Facebook and that we couldn't generate the kind of capital needed to quickly promote a stand-alone gaming destination. We designed our technology so that it would plug in as an application to their platform, and that became the driver for the integrated Facebook application.
	We then created another application that allowed those who weren't Facebook members to participate.
	Finally, we used Facebook advertising to target our customers, and it was so successful that for a time we had turn off the ads because our site couldn't handle the traffic.
What talent and resources will you need to engage?	I am not a gaming programmer, nor do I have experience as an educator, so the first thing that I needed was someone who had that experience and could balance my business strengths.
	I began asking around and looking for a chief technical partner. My initial outreach to him was in a cold call, and we started talking. Eventually, he joined me as a partner.
	The second thing we needed to do was identify the content we couldn't—or didn't need to—create on our own and put together the strategy for aggregating existing content for our site.

You can read more about Jane's story in Chapter 9.

> **CURIOSITY, INTUITION, & WEAVING**
>
> *In this phase, women are not only leveraging their Curiosity and Intuition, but also actively (and avidly) Weaving—making connections to other people, services, and ideas that can fuel their ViBIs. Women will typically see more partners than competitors at this stage. One reason is that women are experts at creating allies, partners, and collaborators, and are focused on problem solving with the long term in mind.*

Connect

Now start connecting the ideas for your business with other ideas.

> - What did you learn from the "see" process in the previous section that will help you network with potential partners?
> - How will you connect with the communities, ideas, and people who can help you broaden your perspective and ensure your business model is relevant to your market?

This is the brainstorm phase, and it allows for free association that can enable you to broaden your network and get a handle on obstacles and competitors. When you connect your idea to people doing similar things, you also validate that there is a market for your business.

Creating a Word Cloud

One exercise we've found very helpful in this regard is the **word cloud**. Keep a notebook with you, and every time you talk to other people about

your idea, write down what they say, along with the words they spark in you. You'll soon have a list of meaningful words that later can help you refine and articulate your idea to the outside world and turn it into a compelling **value proposition** for your ViBI. A value proposition is a short, concise statement explaining what differentiates your product or service. We will discuss this further in Chapter 6.

You will also discover that you will need to enlist the help of others to promote your cause, support your vision, and eliminate obstacles for your business. These people are sometimes referred to as **stakeholders** because they have some kind of interest or concern in your business. A helpful tool that can help you identify and then engage with stakeholders is called the **Stakeholder Map**.

Exercise 2: Creating Your Stakeholder Map

1. **Primary stakeholders**: On a blank sheet of paper, draw a circle in the middle and write the name of your business in it. Then, with your business in the center, make a list of the most important people to the success of your business. They can include customers, vendors, partners, staff, members of the media, government and legal decision makers, investors—anyone who is associated with or has a perception of your brand or business. These are your "primary stakeholders." Place these in circles around your central circle, and draw lines to connect them to your business.

2. **Secondary stakeholders**: Now ask yourself, who or what influences your primary stakeholders? These are your secondary stakeholders. Place them in circles around the appropriate primary-stakeholder circles, and draw lines between them and make connections to visualize how your stakeholders are connected.

3. **Critical priorities**: Next, draw rectangles around or highlight those stakeholders who are most critical to the success of your business.

An illustration follows of how your completed Stakeholder Map should look. Remember, each map will vary; there's no "correct" number of primary stakeholders to have, or number of secondary stakeholders each primary stakeholder should have. Your map will be unique, as it will reflect your unique business proposition, environment, and network.

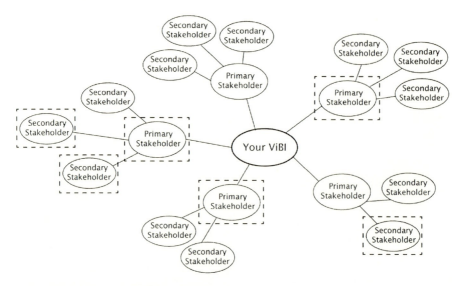

Reaching Your Stakeholders

Once you have identified your stakeholders, the next step is to determine how you will reach them. For each stakeholder, ask yourself four questions:

› How do I know them?
› What is their potential impact on my business?
› What aspect of my business can help or harm them?
› What do I want to ask them to do?

Make a list and keep track of the people you come across within your existing network, and more important, those you meet within new networks. Join industry associations like the National Association of Women Business Owners (NAWBO) and your local Chamber of Commerce. Seek out people who have started their own successful businesses and pick their brains. Eventually, you will find invaluable resources, guides, and women's entrepreneurial networks.

In our research and interviews, we have found that women often have a difficult time asking others for help. One entrepreneurial group we know in Boston begins every meeting by allowing all members to "share their asks." By making it acceptable and safe for members to ask for what they need, this group is sharing the resources and research that make valuable the time they spend networking.

Every time you have a conversation about your business, ask if that person knows anyone else you should talk with. Then, follow up right away with that introduction. Evaluate how and where you are networking. If you're talking about your ViBI only to friends and family, you will miss the connections you need. At the same time, if you're spending all your time at networking events that don't lead to interesting and useful connections, your valuable time may be better spent elsewhere.

> **WEAVING & PASSION**
>
> *In this step, you rely heavily on Weaving as you connect and thread together your network and make connections for your idea with stakeholders, customers, and potential partners. Passion plays a critical role because you have to talk about your business to an external audience over and over again, asking and answering questions and thinking through how your business connects with a view to the broader community. The more passionate you are about your idea, the more compelling and confident you will be.*

Analyze

Now it is time to analyze, associate, and apply what you've learned to your business plan, associating and comparing your business model to other meaningful businesses. Apply critical thinking to validate and clarify what is unique about your ViBI.

Look at your customers' profiles and needs and what your competitors currently offer. What would make your service or product different and better? Can you identify a sweet spot in that intersection of needs and abilities?

The SWOT Analysis

A **SWOT analysis** is a quick tool for synthesizing what you've learned so far. This common tool identifies the **Strengths** and **Weaknesses** of your business model and your approach. You also look at the **Opportunities** that you've uncovered and what **Threats** you will have to overcome. You can do a SWOT analysis for many aspects of your business. Every time you complete a SWOT analysis, you can go back to your ViBI and improve it, refine it, and make it more specific.

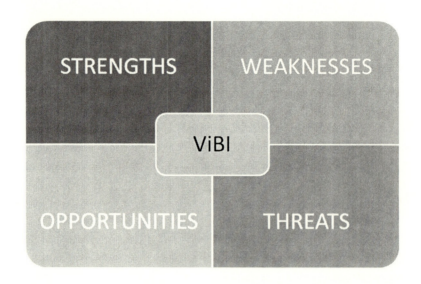

> **INTUITION & CREATIVITY**
>
> *What you find in the analysis stage may be invigorating, frustrating, or both, depending on your idea and the saturation of your market. When you start to uncover real roadblocks, rely on your Intuition and Creativity to help you strengthen your value proposition and define your own approach.*

Nest

The final stage is one that many people overlook. Giving yourself time to digest what you have learned and begin to organize your thoughts will result in better decisions about what to change and what to leave in your business model. Nesting is creating a space for yourself (and your business) to nurture and grow. By "nurture," we mean the conscious act of creating a mental incubator where your idea can sprout and take root. Nesting your business allows you to do the same visualization we do when preparing for a baby or creating a new home space for yourself or your family: When you begin to visualize yourself in that setting, that context, and that future, you create room for action.

Nesting, Part 1

Wrap it all up by envisioning your business as a collective whole:

› What are my objectives?
› Is my vision clear?
› Who are my customers?
› What will I sell to them?
› Why will they buy it?
› How will we make money?
› What is our supply chain and partnership model?
› What will this business look like next month? next year? five years from now?

Choosing to write this book was the logical nesting process for the SmartGirls Way vision. Prior to writing it, Jean had started developing the SmartGirls Way business plan. It just so happened that she was ready to launch at the very worst part of the economic crisis. She had to decide if she wanted to spend two years and a great deal of resources getting venture capital on board with the business model—or spend her efforts elsewhere. She realized that continuing down this path would require her to change her vision to meet one version after another of potential investors' ideal models. However, the SCAN process told her there was a real gap in the support and empowerment of women entrepreneurs, and that adjusted her approach to her vision in a different way: She could write a book and organize a movement of other successful women who were working the SmartGirls Way.

Nesting, Part 2

Nesting is also about making the plans you need to align your business with your life:

| What is *my* time-table? *How long* will it take? What **MILESTONES** and **deadlines** will I set? | What are the things I *have to prioritize*, **STOP**, or put on hold while I focus on MY BUSINESS? | *Where* and *when* AM I going to **work on my business?** | Who do I need to ENGAGE to *help me* WITH my business— at home, *at work*? |

Entrepreneurs are notorious for jumping into things with both feet. These questions clarify the implications and consequences of your business and help you understand the trade-offs you need to make and/or the support systems you need to put in place to be successful.

> **INTUITION & INTEGRITY**
>
> *Nesting is very much an Intuition and Integrity exercise. This is the time to put some distance between yourself and "the data" and allow that inner voice to speak. If you are passionate about your ViBI, it will be easy and exciting to visualize your business and its future, and you'll need to temper that with your Integrity to make sure you can achieve balance and alignment with the rest of your life.*

Remember, to complete the exercises in this chapter as well as more exercises to help you develop your ViBI, visit SmartGirlsWay.com to purchase the *SmartGirls Way Workbook*.

6

FOCUS

The previous chapter gave you a big-picture view of your business. When we transition into the FOCUS stage, we are able take that outcome of the SCAN's broad landscape and direct it toward the launch of your business into the world.

FOCUS stands for **F**ind your relevancy, **O**rganize and **C**ommit to action, **U**nderwrite yourself, and **S**tart! This is the **action element** of your business plan and a critical part to understand and articulate as you begin sharing with potential partners and investors.

While we don't wish to downplay its importance, over the years, we have seen many an entrepreneur get caught up in the exercise of perfecting the business plan to the point that it becomes an inhibitor to actually starting the business. We have also seen many women jump into an endeavor because they have a tremendous Passion and vision, but fail to think through a concrete plan for getting there.

The SmartGirls Way FOCUS steps are created to provide you with the information you'll need to create the core of your business plan. They outline the thinking and actions required to turn your ViBI into a business.

Find Your Relevancy

The first step in FOCUS is to *find your relevancy* within your marketplace.

> *How will I stand out, grab attention, or just*
> *plain reach the right people I need to succeed?*

To start, you can use the thinking and analysis from the previous chapter to create a **value proposition**. A value proposition helps you articulate *what it is you want to be known for.* It is the start of your business plan, and from this, you build all of your objectives and set forward your intentions for how you will launch and grow your vision.

In Chapter 5, you started to outline your path to market. Now it is time to focus in on every step your business goes through, from raw materials/intellectual capital to the eventual end user. In the traditional business world, the goal of the value chain is to deliver *maximum value* for *the least possible total cost*—and it typically has six components:

1. Who are your target customers?
2. What is the real and perceived value of their experience with you?
3. What are the products and solutions will you provide?
4. What are the benefits?
5. What makes you different from others?
6. How will you validate your business concept and deliver it to market?

Heidi Ganahl, founder of the $50 million doggie day-care franchise Camp Bow Wow, defines value in two ways: the service level (her animal and human customers), and the social impact (creating a new category of pet care that would improve the lives of animals).

"I based my business model and customer profile on what I wanted for my own pets. Doggie day cares were just taking off around the country, and none of them offered boarding solutions," she says. "If you were going to travel away from your pets, your only options were the standard indoor/outdoor doggie runs that offered maybe two outdoor play sessions a day, or the sterile crate options offered by the local veterinarian. The third option was pet sitters, but often this meant your animal was alone for long periods throughout the day."

So Heidi set out to provide the ultimate away-from-home camp for pets. Her goal was to create a safe, fun, and successful environment where dogs could play with other dogs.

She priced her service about 25 percent higher than other boarding solutions and focused the value of service as her key differentiator. "We had a saying, 'Don't put the dollar before the dog,' and it was the value on which we based our staff training, our franchise agreements, and our brand to be a top-notch facility that was leagues better than what was currently out there," she says.

Heidi's business model centered on a premier care offering: "It wasn't a 'frou-frou' spa experience, but a real camp in a state-of-the-art facility that had all of the safety and technology aspects that made the experience easy and accessible, such as a Web camera so you can see what your pets are doing at any time, and online billing."

From the very beginning, Heidi made a conscious choice to go beyond providing a service and dedicated a large portion of her time and efforts toward furthering the cause of animals nationwide. Through the Bow Wow Buddies Foundation, she established a way to take what she learned about building ultimate pet facilities and shared that knowledge in the form of fund-raising, fostering, events, and the support of research and education.

Proof and validation for her concept came from ongoing feedback from customers and the demand to scale. "When I opened the second location eighteen months later, it went really well and ramped up even quicker," she says. "Nine months later, we were asked to create a facility in Troy, Michigan, and it was the beginning of our franchise model."

Here is how Heidi's **value chain** would have looked at the end of 2000 when she was opening the first Camp Bow Wow in Denver, Colorado.

Your Value Chain
Heidi Ganahl, Camp Bow Wow

Customer target: Who are you targeting?

Busy pet owners searching for a day-care and boarding solution for their pets.

They are busy professionals or families who travel, have access to technology, and want an easy-to-access, worry-free environment they can feel good about.

Value experience: What is the value experience (real and perceived) for that customer?

Safety for the dog (and the staff).

Over-the-top customer service that takes care of the pet and the human client.

State-of-the-art facility that brings new meaning to animal care.

> **Product/solution:** What is the product or service mix you're selling, and what makes it cost-competitive?
>
> *Premier care:* Boarding and day care in a top-notch facility that is clean, safe, and—most of all—full of fun. Pets can have a safe place of their own and enjoy ongoing interaction and play with other furry friends and humans who look after their needs.
>
> *Extraordinary service:* Individual attention, easy-to-use services (online check-in and checkout, automatic payment and billing, watch and check up on your pet anytime you want via webcam or mobile device, grooming and nail services).
>
> *Totally fun:* Camp theme of all-day playtime and campfire treats at night add to the whimsical brand experience.
>
> *Safety first:* Supervised play ensures it is easy to separate the dogs and keep them in a setting where they remain calm. Comprehensive staff training in dog behavior and disease management.
>
> **Benefits:** What are the benefits to the community and world?
>
> Gives customers a better option for their pets.
>
> People who couldn't have pets before (because of a busy lifestyle) can now adopt, own, and enjoy a life with animals.
>
> All of our facilities foster animals and work with shelters in local communities to socialize and make them more adoptable.
>
> Give back via our Bow Wow Buddies Foundation—devoted to fund-raising, adoption, and cancer research.
>
> **Alternatives/differentiators:** What makes your business different from your competitors?
>
> We provide access and an all-day "experience" that a sterile vet clinic, standard dog-run boarding, or absentee care cannot provide.
>
> **Validation:** How will you deliver?
>
> Meet the existing gap in pet care.
>
> Solicit feedback on an ongoing basis.
>
> Deliver a scalable model that I can franchise.

When you can answer these questions, you're ready to create your value proposition. In a SmartGirls Way context, your value proposition goes beyond identifying your value to your customer. It also helps you assess the Integrity impact of your brand by answering the question, *What do I want to be known for?*

The following is how Heidi funneled her value chain into a value proposition.

Your Value Proposition
Heidi Ganahl, Camp Bow Wow

> **I want to be known for:**
> We want to be the best-choice care provider for your pet when you can't be there and provide a healthy, happy, and safe environment where a dog can be a dog.

To complete the exercises in this chapter as well as more exercises to help you develop your ViBI, visit SmartGirlsWay.com to purchase the *SmartGirls Way Workbook*.

> ### INTEGRITY, INTUITION, & CURIOSITY
> *Your value proposition is a very personal thing, and it will be largely be derived from your Integrity. Your Intuition will help you internally validate your value proposition. Curiosity works as the amplifier strength for your Integrity and Intuition as you work to find your relevancy. Be open and seek help from partners if necessary.*

Organize for Action

Organize for action is the next stage of FOCUS. Things start to get exciting when you become organized, because it gives you a sense of purpose and accomplishment. We suggest you begin to organize for action by answering two questions:

1. What do I *need* for my product or service?
2. How do I enlist *support* for my ViBI?

Identifying Needs

Sometimes, when you look at all you need to do, it can be daunting. To avoid giving into feeling overwhelmed, create a complete to-do list of everything you can think of, and then organize it by category and divide into priority chunks.

Remember the story from Chapter 3 of Elizabeth Bennett, founder of Africa Direct? Like many women just starting out, Elizabeth's biggest need for her family *and* her business was cash. Upon returning to the States, the first thing she and her partner did was to have a yard sale to sell whatever of the African crafts they could. The feedback from that sale gave Elizabeth a sense of which goods people were most attracted to and how much they would be willing to pay for them. This became Elizabeth's first market-research project. It also helped her identify her first sales channel: shows and art festivals (it would be two years later before she would migrate her business model to the then-burgeoning eBay).

Another top priority was getting the appropriate human resources aligned. Elizabeth needed to identify who was going to be making the products and who was going to handle the logistics involved in bringing them to market. She also needed to decide on her business format and balance near- and long-term needs. For example, she could easily set up her business as a sole proprietorship, so rather than hiring lawyers to incorporate her early business, she spent her time and resources on securing a resale license that would enable her to purchase her goods less expensively and also set her up to charge and collect tax.

Prioritizing Your Needs

	Capital	Supply Chain	Legal	Marketing	Operations
Step #1	Find quick cash. Identify business costs and personal family needs	Secure retail license	Choose and register business name	Identify sales channel	Decide business format
Step #2		Human resources for unit production		Determine pricing	Source African traders
Step #3				Create signs and show collateral	Define business mission and concept

Your needs will be very different from Elizabeth's. It doesn't matter what your categories are as long as they help you *organize* and *focus*.

The second part of organizing for action is identifying the **Champions**, **Cheerleaders**, and **Collaborators** you need to enlist to launch your business, and creating intentional, win-win agreements. This goes beyond connecting and networking; it involves asking people to do something—give money or commit time, sweat equity, or pro-bono advice.

Looking at your Stakeholder Map from Chapter 5, you can probably identify a number of people you need to enlist.

Champions, Cheerleaders, and Collaborators

> *Champions* are those who may serve as good advocates to your business. You may want them to act as spokespersons or members of your advisory board—and perhaps, ultimately, investors.
>
> *Cheerleaders* are those whose opinions and word of mouth can make or break your business. Often, these are your best customers and early adopters of your product, service, or solution.
>
> *Collaborators* are those you entrust to help you grow and execute your business. They may be employees or business partners. *And* they are your domestic partners, parents, children, and child-care providers, those who are fundamental to your overall work/life balance.

For many women, launching a dream business involves trade-offs. A trade-off can be taking on a partner or selling shares in your business. It may mean you have to invest your personal nest egg as seed money until you grow big enough to attract an investor. A trade-off will almost always require short-term changes in your home life and income. Whatever the trade-off, it needs to be a choice that you—and your supporters—can live with.

You must create an "and-and" rather than an "either-or" dialogue with all three of these types of supporters and have frequent conversations with each, keeping the following in mind:

> › **Be very clear about your needs and what you will do to honor and respect your supporters' time, investments, and efforts**. If you are asking potential partners to join your venture in sweat equity, formalize your agreements and be clear up front about the risks,

rewards, and expectations. If you're asking a Champion to make an introduction or provide an endorsement, be prompt and responsive, and find ways to pay it forward (or back, as the case may be).

› **Be clear about your motivations in asking for help, and do so in a way that is genuine and respectful of the relationship.** Women in business settings sometimes have a difficult time being assertive, and this discomfort can result in the impression of being too aggressive or too passive. In his book *The Seven Habits of Highly Effective People*, Steven Covey talks about the importance of clarity around a goal and the strength of relationships in creating win-win conversations. It is absolutely essential that you have the confidence to ask for what you need.[1]

This most often plays out in personal relationships. When the push and urgency of your business begins to heat up, you'll often find the most difficult interactions come with those closest to you—your spouse, friends, and the employees you depend on to reach your goals. Creating ongoing conversations and "check-in" points with these caretakers of your business is essential for developing "and-and" relationships.

Two of the least understood differences between men and women in the workplace is how we seek solutions and who gets the credit. Libba Pinchot is the cofounder of the Bainbridge Graduate Institute, one of the first sustainable business schools in the United States. Pinchot defines a **sustainable business** as "living for the greatest good." In the past, she says, men were acknowledged for their abilities to be strong and capable providers. They claimed and received credit for their conquests and accomplishments with land, wealth, and legacy. Women, meanwhile, as the bearers of children, cared more about creating success within the community. Women were historically more focused on finding the water source that would nurture the tribe than getting credit for it.

One of the ways that women are great at creating an "and-and" dialogue is through seeking solutions *first*. There will be times as you build your business when your ego will play a large role in some of these interactions. You need to strike a balance between *honoring* and *claiming* what you have created and "giving some of your business away" to other partners and investors in order to see your greatest dreams realized.

Knowing when to acknowledge yourself as well as when to put aside ego for a greater good is an important skill.

> **PASSION, INTEGRITY, & INTUITION**
>
> *Passion and Integrity are strong players in organizing for action. If you're optimizing your Passion, it will drive to you implement, pushing you out of bed in the morning with an excitement and sense of urgency to act. Your Integrity and Intuition will guide you in the "and-and" dialogues and relationships you will need to foster with your supporters.*

Commit to Action

Many entrepreneurs never get out of the planning phases because they become obsessed with or overwhelmed by perfecting their business plans. If you don't make a commitment to action, your dream will always be just that: a dream.

We suggest four steps to help you commit to your action. Completing each step moves you one step further on your path to launching your entrepreneurial dream.

Make Your First Move

Every woman entrepreneur we have talked with can pinpoint the moment or catalyst that propelled her to take that big, scary leap.

Telling her story to other people enabled Sarah McIlroy to leave her successful career working for brand-name game publishers. "When I first started to pitch FashionPlaytes, everyone embraced the idea, but potential investors wanted to see how we could actually produce custom designs at a reasonable price point. I needed to find someone who could help me with the back-end production and prove we could build out and scale that end of the business," she says.

So, Sarah's first move for FashionPlaytes was to find a cofounder who would bring not just experience but the credibility needed to attract her investors. "I knew *how* I wanted to handle the production, but I didn't have any of the connections in manufacturing that [cofounder] Mary Beth Tirrell brought to FashionPlaytes. Proving out the production process gave us the credibility we needed to get funded," she says.

Your stimulus may be a trade show, a launch event, a conversation with a future partner or potential investor, or the creation of a website. Once you put yourself out there with an *intention* to start a business, it is like tossing a rock into the pond: The resulting ripple can be the beginning of a wave of recognition, discovery, and success.

But a catalyst is not enough. You actually have to *commit* to continue. Your first move is in many ways the trickiest part. It's the entrepreneurial equivalent of your first bike ride without the training wheels. In the same way that pedaling first generates the energy and drive to stay in motion, progress is the key to success and action is the fuel your business needs.

Set Aggressive Goals

Once you've picked a starting point, you need to solidify your commitment by putting a stake in the ground. Set aggressive—even audacious—goals and set dates around them. Then tell someone. Once you've made a commitment to someone other than yourself, you are more accountable to make it happen. Will this increase your stress? Yes, but in a good way. Not only does accountability help you move forward, it provides direction and helps engage others' support. Whether you are energizing and mobilizing a team, seeking funding, or creating relationships in an evolving supply chain, your vocal intention and aggressive goals help others sense your commitment to action and get caught up in your Passion. There is a significant difference between "what I'd like to do *someday*" and "what I am going to do *today*."

Creating a mindset of intention is what Sheryl O'Loughlin and her co-founder Neil Grimmer set out to do with Nest Collective, an organic-food company providing nourishing food for children "from the high chair to the lunch box." Nest Collective's social mission was to turn the tide on the childhood obesity crisis by nourishing kids and helping them to develop a lifetime joy of healthy eating. To reach this aggressive goal, they set out to acquire small, existing brands with big opportunity. Nest would leverage that opportunity through design innovation.

They acquired Plum Organics, a pioneer in frozen baby food and a leading provider of premium organic foods for babies and toddlers. They also purchased the consumer products division of Revolution Foods, a company focused on providing healthy lunch food for kids. Both companies already had a devoted consumer base and high food integrity, and together allowed Nest to focus on its high-chair-to-lunch-box target demographic. However, the product experience with both companies wasn't meeting the busy lifestyles of modern parents and kids.

Next, Sheryl and Neil focused their collective talent for innovation and product design to improve the overall consumer experience with these products. By changing how the organic baby-food line was prepared and packaged, they were able to create an entirely new category of baby and toddler food that tasted great and met the busy lifestyles of modern parents and kids. Under the Revolution brand, the Nest team also introduced a portable lunch-box line of organic, nourishing food that both kids and parents could feel good about.

As Sheryl explains, "When you're starting out as an entrepreneur, it is important to understand yourself and where you add value better than anyone in the world. We gave up a big chunk of our ownership to partner with venture capitalists who would help us to grow our business and accomplish our mission quickly. Purchasing these great brands allowed us to focus on what we were really good at—innovation and design. It enabled us to enter the market rapidly, experiment, see what was working and what wasn't, and build on it. Setting an aggressive goal helped us stay focused on the social mission of making life better for parents and kids."

Energize Your Team

By energizing your team, you create a force-multiplier for your early business. The commitment to action requires a commitment to pace, and it will take others to keep the pace. Whether it is vendors, partners, or employees, you will find that engaging others in your progress, keeping them appraised as you evolve your ViBI, and finding ways for them to be a part of the action will cement your commitment.

One way to create a sense of shared commitment and energize your team is to develop shared language, symbols, and typology. That may come from the question, *What do I want to be known for*? Name it, talk about it, and visualize it with your logo or slogan. When Dream Dinners began to franchise nationwide, Stephanie Allen and her cofounder, Tina Kuna, wanted to be known as the company that nurtured moms so they in turn could nurture their families.

"In the early days of our expansion, we wanted to make sure that we had nurturing people, so we put that in the franchise application. Even today, the first question on our franchise application asks them: *If you could wave a magic wand and change the world, what would you do?* We wanted to know how those potential franchisees wanted to make a difference, and we even called it the Magic Wand application," explains Stephanie.

As the business grew, Stephanie and Tina struggled with the influx of competing franchises that modeled themselves after their idea.

"We created an industry, and then people started copying our idea," Stephanie says. "We got a bit too focused on competition instead of focusing on what we do and doing it best. You can't patent big ideas, but you can create a culture that really distinguishes you from the rest."

Realizing that their efforts were best spent on choosing the right franchisees who were in alignment with the Dream Dinners mission, Stephanie and Tina wove together a new community that now serves 700,000 meals a month.

Face Your Fears

A common reason women don't start their own companies is the fear of failure.[2] Yes, it's scary. And yes, you could fail...but you could also learn something along the way. There are many reasons that people should not become entrepreneurs. However, we believe that if you've come this far in the process, chances are you're feeling an internal drive to birth your business. At this point, the only thing stopping you may be that first move—and that move is up to you!

After Michelle King Robson founded EmpowHER, she had a moment of doubt and uncertainty about her qualifications to lead.

"I always regretted that I didn't have a college education, yet as I started this company, I wasn't going to let anything get in my way," Michelle says. "After three years of running EmpowHER, it became very apparent that here I was struggling to give underserved women a voice, and I realized that the one person who didn't have a voice was *me*. I didn't really own my own voice in the company because I didn't think I was as qualified, and felt that there were others who could do this better than me."

Michelle realized that she needed to embrace herself for *who she was* instead of focusing on *who she was not*. Her qualifier was the seed of the ViBI that she had nurtured and grown into a successful company. "Overcoming this fear allowed me to 'own' my own voice and surround myself with people who will push me and elevate me to where we want to be. When I took ownership of the goal and embraced my expertise, I empowered myself to lead."

The **FUD factor**—**F**ear, **U**ncertainty, and **D**oubt—is essentially a common term for "appealing to your fears." You will encounter pessimists and others who tell you your business idea is impossible, and that can weaken your motivation. But if you've intentionally gone through the SCAN process and you are genuinely (and passionately) excited about your business, you will have the stamina to persevere. Whatever you do, don't let the FUD factor prevent you from recognizing your call to action for your business launch and then committing to making it happen.

PASSION

Achieving these goals will often involve other people, so you will need to draw upon your Passion to energize your team and keep them motivated.

Underwrite Yourself

Our discussions of the SCAN and FOCUS processes should help you answer the question, *Is this business viable?* One of the most critical determinants of this is how you will *fund your business.*

Starting a business is akin to birthing and nurturing a baby. One budding entrepreneur we spoke with explained it this way: "It's like making a commitment and a financial obligation to raising a baby who can't tell you that it loves you for two years. Then all of a sudden it is walking and talking and soon it takes on a life of its own and grows up."

Just as there are stages of growth for your company, there are also stages of capital. When you begin to look at the creation of your business as a life cycle, it can help you identify and make decisions about the financial requirements and opportunities available to you.

Remember, you are not just funding a business, you are underwriting yourself. This mind-set can help you keep perspective during the roller-coaster experience that all entrepreneurs encounter.

In the early days of our "first move," we set out to find and celebrate the stories of 100 women entrepreneurs in 100 days. We call this initiative the 100x100 Project. One of the first people we met was a very wise woman by the name of Sharon Lechter. Sharon is a celebrated author, is the founder and CEO of Pay Your Family First, was a member of the inaugural President's Advisory Council on Financial Literacy, and is presently a member of the American Institute of CPAs' Commission on Financial Literacy. Her efforts to educate women and girls about managing their financial wealth in a thoughtful and informed way have taught her the importance of tenacity and persistence when securing the start-up funding that women entrepreneurs need to be successful.

"My advice is to have faith in yourself and your mission, and to keep trying; don't give up. This timeless phrase holds real meaning in creating a successful business and life. Persistence is and always will be the leading trait of successful people. So many people quit just steps away success. But the persistent person knows that no matter how many times they may trip, stumble or fail, persistence will carry them on to a new day, a new project and a waiting success," says Sharon. "Whenever you face obstacles or doubt, know that persistence will carry you through."

Being resolute in actions and proper planning are important foundations to keep in mind as you underwrite yourself and your business. Building on this, we have three SmartGirls Way rules:

1. Support yourself first.
2. Validate your business plan.
3. Find your bankroll.

Rule #1: Support Yourself First

Part of the reason women fear going into business for themselves can be linked to two common myths.

> *Myth #1: Choosing to be an entrepreneur is a hard and difficult choice between family and business.*

Recent studies indicate that women with children of all ages are working more hours than ever before, and they're doing so at great personal sacrifice, spending more time at work and less time in community and civic involvement, leisure time, and even sleep.[3] But it doesn't have to be this way. When you create a business that is aligned with vision and leverages your core strengths, you may find yourself spending significant time focused on that business. This is common and a good thing—when you're feeling energized and aligned in your work, it has a positive impact on the other aspects of your life as well. As your business grows and succeeds, you will realize that there is now more time available to spend with your family and realize the long-term benefit of being a successful entrepreneur. You have built an asset (your business) that works for you!

Along the pathway to success, focused business time also contributes to the creation of a schedule and practices that will allow you to take defined breaks from work to spend time with your family—as well as defined breaks from your family to spend time on your work. The key to balanced success is clear transitions and discipline to stick to your schedule.

While balance has always been, and will continue to be, a challenge for working women, owning your own business means that you can find ways to include your family in your ViBI to make it rewarding for everyone. Involving your children has the added benefit of introducing them early to entrepreneurship and the benefits that business ownership can mean in their lives.

Another way you can support yourself is through the camaraderie and learning that comes through connecting with other women. Women are three times more likely to be involved in early-stage entrepreneurship if we already have a job, which means that our next investor or collaborator may very well be in some peer group we are already connected to. There are a number of women's entrepreneurial organizations and incubator groups across the country *looking* for more women to add to their collaborative "think-and-do" tanks. A support system comprised of other entrepreneurs can help you create a supportive infrastructure in which you will find not only the encouragement you need, but many of the answers and key relationships that will ensure your success. Napoleon Hill, author of *Think and Grow Rich* and *Outwitting the Devil*, called this type of a support system a "Mastermind Alliance," and highlighted its importance for entrepreneurs wanting to create and realize their greatest success.[4]

> *Myth #2: You will have to go into debt or "give away" most of your business to venture capitalists to start a company.*

We strongly discourage any woman from bankrolling her company by maxing out her charge cards or leveraging her mortgage to the hilt. You need to always pay yourself and your family first.

It is important not to become overly zealous in how you fund your business at any stage, especially in the early stages. That doesn't mean you don't seek out seed funding. It does mean that you go into any agreement with eyes open and a view of the long-term impact on your business. Over the years, we have seen entrepreneurs (male *and* female) make decisions that may bring short-term capital at the expense of long-term impact on control and alignment. This is particularly true when it comes to equity financing.

Raising capital at any stage requires confidence and letting go of any **scarcity mentality** you may have about money. Many attribute lack of confidence as a reason that less than 8 percent of all venture capital goes to women entrepreneurs. The venture-capital model romanticized by the Mark Zuckerberg–like stories contribute to an enduring misperception that because women are more conservative in how they invest and spend, they don't make good entrepreneurs.[5] This is **legacy thinking** that implies that women are risk-averse. But the very fact that women are *so responsible* about debt makes them a good risk—they are committed to meeting their obligations.

There are numerous forms of finance models—equity, debt, and combinations—with new hybrids evolving every day. As the one who is ultimately responsible for your businesses success, you need to understand fully how any option aligns with your business stage, your values, and your awareness of what that money actually represents.

If you take on capital, you'll need to pay particular attention to term sheets and how to negotiate them. They will affect not only your share of the business, but your future say in your business. This is a subject that could fill an entire book, and we will be focusing on how to navigate the fund-raising playing field in future publications.

For now, Sharon Lechter advises: "Seek advice, choose investors, align with positive associations, and take risks that are in alignment with the Integrity of your vision. The amount of money that you seek, timing, and nature of your fundraising efforts can make all of the difference between retaining control of your company and giving away the store."

Sharon explains that funding can take a number of different forms, each with its own advantages and disadvantages, and they can generally be categorized in three ways:

1. Self-Funding and Leveraging There are a number of alternatives to the classical fund-raising models. In recent years, the growth of strategic equity partners has been successful for many entrepreneurs. In this model, you directly negotiate an exchange of resources (expertise, manpower, services, and products) that you need to grow your business for much better terms than you could obtain raising cash and then paying for the resource. Another example is leveraging intellectual property assets for your own products through licensing strategies to create cash flows.

"Self-funding may simply not be an option; not everybody can afford to self-fund a company or wait to accumulate the necessary funds, particularly when they have to take action within a finite window of opportunity," adds Sharon. "However, if self-funding is feasible, it is the simplest and least expensive way to raise capital. You retain complete ownership of your company and all of the benefits of success. However, you also assume all the risk."

2. Debt Financing Capital from other people or entities always has a price tag—although it is often well worth the price: "When you take a loan, you typically pay interest," Sharon explains. "The typically inflexible requirement to repay principal plus interest can sometimes present cash-flow management difficulties in an emerging business. However, debt financing, like self-funding, allows you to retain complete ownership of the company, though sometimes subject to restrictive covenants or lender oversight."

In short, you not only receive all of the benefits of success, but ultimately, the loan will be paid off. And like self-funding, you retain all the risk of failure; in most cases, you will have to pay off the loan even if the business fails.

3. Equity Funding When you sell **equity**, the price you pay for the capital is a percentage of the ownership of your company. The specific percentage of the company that you have to give to the investor for each dollar raised is a function of the valuation of your company at the time you sell the equity. This is why the amount of funding sought and the timing of equity offerings are critical. You need to parse your equity offerings into **tranches** (portions) corresponding to upward steps in the valuation of your company.

Ideally, you raise only enough money in each offering tranche to get you to the next step in valuation. If you raise too much money through equity offerings when the valuation of your company is still low, you are likely to lose control of the company. According to Sharon, parsing finance is more work, and has a modicum of risk that money will not be available when you need it, but if done right, can make the difference between retaining control of your company and giving away the store.

If you need more information on capital formation, and particularly, alternatives to the classical approaches to raising capital, we strongly recommend the book *OPM: Other People's Money*, by Sharon's husband and business partner, Michael Lechter.[6] Another book worth taking a look at is *Venture Deals: Be Smarter than Your Lawyer and Venture Capitalist* by Brad Feld and Jason Mendelson.[7]

Rule #2: Validate Your Business Plan

There are many resources and templates available for creating your business plan. For example, the SBA has a template that walks you through the entire business-plan creation, and we encourage you to spend time with this and other tools and examples as you create your own versions.[8] The key is not to let the template or the format intimidate or rule you. It's most important to get your idea down.

Once you have created your business plan, you'll want to run it by outside experts. This is the perfect time to start building your group of "trusted advisors." Seek out experts who bring a different perspective and skill set, and have them review your plan. The people who provide you with radically honest feedback in a constructive way may also make great additions to a formal board of advisors.

In addition to soliciting feedback on your plan, you will likely need to create various formats of that plan to share with different audiences. These can include:

> Your **executive summary** – Outlines the contents of your business plan in such a way that an investor can quickly understand your business model, what you are planning to deliver to the marketplace, why your solution is relevant to your customers, how you plan to operate and market your business, expected revenue, costs, profit and loss, and your timeline for reaching your goals within the next three to five years.

> Your **short story** – Commonly known as the "**elevator pitch**." Used to engage potential investors, customers, or partners in conversation about your business.

> Your **visual pitch** – A presentation you give to engage potential investors to read a full-length presentation. Spend time to ensure that your visual pitch is visually engaging and that it concisely explains your executive summary, your financial plan, key trends and decision- making benchmarks, and a demonstration or example of your product or service.

All of these should give your potential investors an understanding of both the overall value your business provides to the world as well as the "under-the-hood" aspects of how you will operate your business.

For each of these formats, it is helpful to ensure you check off the following components:

Business-Plan Executive-Summary Checklist

- ☑ Description of your business and value proposition
- ☑ Business context (environment you will be operating in, industry trends, and background)
- ☑ Competitive overview
- ☑ Challenges and opportunities (market analysis)
- ☑ Product/service offering differentiators (e.g., intellectual property or exclusive rights) and barriers to competition
- ☑ Path to market (channels, partners, suppliers)
- ☑ Operating plan (how you plan to execute and organize your business)
- ☑ Marketing and sales plan (quick wins)
- ☑ Team (staff, advisors, Champions, and other stakeholders)
- ☑ Financial forecast (projected revenues, costs, balance sheet)
- ☑ Execution and timeline
- ☑ Critical success factors

A note of caution: Make sure you protect yourself and your ideas, and ask the people who review your plan to sign a **nondisclosure agreement (NDA)**. There are several websites that provide affordable nondisclosure-agreement templates. One resource is legalzoom.com.[9] An NDA is a good tool for creating a mutual understanding of privacy and accountability right from the start. It's common for venture capitalists not to sign an NDA, but if you're uncomfortable having them review your plan without one, you probably should not be talking to them.

If you haven't already done so, now is also the time to secure your website, company name, and any relevant copyrights and patents associated with your product and brand. Once you compile a list of any marks you wish to protect, you can conduct a preliminary search on each at www.uspto.gov.[10] For a primer on the intellectual-property protection process, go to www.uspto.gov/trademarks/basics/index.jsp.[11]

Rule #3: Find Your Bankroll

Before you can determine where to access your capital, you need to define how much start-up capital you will require.

Taking into account how much you will charge for your various products and services, you should be able to calculate your expected revenue. Look at this figure from both a short-term and long-term view, which can include events that increase the value of your company such as filling out your leadership team, completion of market studies, proof of principle or market viability for your product or service, completion of prototypes, intellectual-property protection (such as filing trademark and patent applications/grant of trademark registrations and patents), and securing significant contracts (for example, with vendors, distributors, or customers).

As you scale your business (open more channels for reaching and obtaining your customers), you can begin to forecast how that revenue will grow. Most investors look for a plan that forecasts three to five years out.

Next, you will need to determine your operational costs. Make a list of the expenses for your business from office equipment, cost of materials, distribution, office/business space, staff, vendors, marketing activities, insurance, taxes, travel, and other incidentals. When looking at your expenses, you will need to be both creative and prudent about each expense; making a profit will be a challenge at first, and efficiency (but not at the detriment of your goals) is required.

You will undoubtedly encounter additional, unplanned expenses. We've talked with many women entrepreneurs and investors about how to estimate initial start-up cost and received two specific pieces of advice:

1. If you don't have a background in finance, seek guidance from someone who does.

2. When you land on a final estimate, consider doubling that number. There are always unexpected expenses that arise in starting a new business—and the lack of enough capital is one of the main reasons new companies fail.

Once you have an idea of your potential revenue and your initial capital needs, you need to understand the options and stages of funding available to you. Just as there are stages of growth for your company, there are also stages of capital. When you begin to look at the creation of your business as a life cycle, it can help you make decisions.

At any stage, raising capital can be a bit of a balancing act, and there are a variety of funding resources for building and growing a business. Each has its own risks and rewards, and we lay them out here as options to consider.

Start-Up Capital

The first stage is your seed money, or **start-up capital**, and it begins from the moment you sketch out your ViBI on a cocktail napkin until you earn your first dollar. Now it is time to think about how you are going to finance that initial product or service you're delivering.

As Sharon Lechter puts it, "You should be thinking about bringing in the resources that you will need to develop your product or service and get it to the market, right from the beginning. How much can you do on your own? Do you need to bring in someone else for specific skills or expertise? What consideration will you have to give them to get them on your team? What resources—materials, equipment, or facilities—will you need? What consideration will you have to give to get access to those resources? The consideration will sometimes be money, sometimes equity, sometimes a profit interest or royalty, or sometimes some form of exchange. In any event, you need to have a plan."

START-UP CAPITAL OPTION: Bootstrapping
Funding your business through your existing job or personal savings.

If your personal savings and income are also used for other critical issues like household expenses or retirement, create a timeline or deadline for how long you plan to bootstrap your business.

Also, make sure you've reviewed your personal finances to see where you will need to make cuts in your overall lifestyle, income, and savings.

Pros	Cons
Allows you to maintain control of the financial future of your business without incurring any debt or interest against it.	Often means you are splitting your time between your business and your existing job, creating short-term balance issues.
	If you have not properly planned ahead, you could be putting your personal financial situation in jeopardy.

START-UP CAPITAL OPTION: Loans from Friends and Family
Borrowing money from family or friends to get your business started.

Money matters can sometimes have a negative impact on personal relationships. It will be important to be very clear about expectations on both sides. Make sure to legally document what kind of loan you are receiving (a gift in kind or a low-interest loan, for example). If it is a loan with interest, documentation should outline payment terms and collateral.

Even if your loan is a gift, there are tax implications. Make sure you have the right advice from your attorneys and accountants about what documents you need and what is required to be reported to the IRS.

Pros	Cons
Can be gifts in kind or loans with very favorable terms.	Accepting money from family or friends can sometimes give them more control over your business than you may want them to have.
If you find yourself in an unforeseen position with your business, you may have more flexibility.	Borrowing from friends or family can bring in emotional baggage.

START-UP CAPITAL OPTION: Crowd-Funding
An online peer-to-peer contribution model that helps you find a community of small contributors to fund your business without the risks of traditional financing.

Crowd-funding can take the form of technology widgets on your website, which allow supporters and customers to chip in, and campaigns that allow friends and family to kick-start your venture (such as kickstarter.com and IndieGoGo.com).[12] The contributions are either donations, the sale of some form of perk (privilege, or right), or a percentage of income (profit interest or royalty) rather than a loan or sale of equity.

This is a nascent fund-raising model, and it is worth investigating each site before listing. You need good legal advice to be very careful that the offering is not deemed to involve a **security**, which is very broadly defined under the law. If the offering does involve a security, unless the offering fits within very specific exemptions to both federal and state security laws, there can be severe legal ramifications.

Pros	Cons
Since the contributions are not a loan, payments to your contributors are not fixed and depend only upon your success. And because this isn't equity, you give up no control or ownership of your company.	You need to have a compelling cause or offering that appeals to the viral nature of crowd-funding, and this method is usually more effective if you want to kick-start creative campaigns or raise money for social causes.

START-UP CAPITAL OPTION: Sweat Equity

Giving equity in your company in exchange for talent.

Be clear with employees about each partner's financial commitment. If you are giving away equity in your company as a shorter-term commitment for a longer-term payoff, you need to draw up legal papers that show how each equity member of the company fits into your organization (such as a principal partner). If you agree that employees are doing the work pro bono, know that the IRS does not generally allow pro-bono efforts to be declared as a loss on your (or their) tax returns.

Pros	Cons
Provides you with the support and resources to get your business off the ground.	Your "talent" may put paying work ahead of your needs.
	Your talent's needs may change over the years.
	You also need to deal with the possibility of a departure by the talent. There are typically testing and sell-back provisions in the agreement with the talent.

Early-Stage Capital

You move out of start-up into **early-stage capital** once you have determined you have a viable product, identified your target market, articulated the relevancy of your product or service to your customers and the marketplace, and done the financial and research due diligence required for your business plan. Early-stage capital is often needed to build the infrastructure to handle sales or deliver your service. This is the point (if you haven't already done it) at which you need to put together your financial forecast of revenue (what you'll bring in), operational costs (expenses and costs you will have to cover), and growth strategy (when you plan to make a profit and how you will grow that profit over time).

EARLY-STAGE CAPITAL OPTION: Personal Loans

You negotiate a monthly rate with interest terms against a personal line of credit or asset.

Personal loans require qualified assets or an income stream, and the best advice is to seek advice from a certified public accountant who will help you look at your overall financial picture. Over the last few years, banks have become stricter about what qualifies for a loan, but they are still in the business of interest and debt, so it is important to look at the interest rate and terms so you can decide if the extra interest you would pay on a loan could be better spent funneling that interest into your business and the maturing of your idea.

If you're leveraging a personal loan for a brick-and-mortar company, beware: There may be a lien by the bank that affects later-stage capital.

Pros	Cons
Banks will often loan larger amounts of money, and this can be a good resource if you're purchasing a storefront or some kind of brick-and-mortar establishment.	Bank loans are increasingly difficult to secure. If your business grows too slowly, you may have to default on your vehicle or real estate, or declare bankruptcy.
The terms of the loan and your expectations to repay it are usually clear and straightforward from the beginning.	

EARLY-STAGE CAPITAL OPTION: Peer-to-Peer and Micro-Lending

Also known as "social lending," individuals borrow and lend money without an intermediary financial institution.

This type of funding is growing in popularity with investors who receive income in the form of interest at better terms than their money would receive in a bank account.

There are many newly structured entrepreneurial fund-raising sites where you can dictate your terms and how you want to pay back your investors (MicroVentures, Profounder, and Prosper.com, for example).[13] While considered a more creative solution for raising capital, this is still a very early experiment, and traditional financial regulations have not yet caught up to this new model of doing business. Several micro-lending sites have recently received cease-and-desist orders, so it is important to do your research before choosing this approach.

Pros	Cons
Removes the middleman from the process.	Usually involves smaller amounts of money.
Can be facilitated through a third-party and can be an excellent source of further investment if you are successful.	Involves more time and risk on the part of investors.
	In some cases, loans may fall within the scope of the securities laws.

EARLY-STAGE CAPITAL OPTION: Small Business Administration Loans

Loans provided by banks for small businesses where the government acts as guarantor.

Businesses must be owner-operated, for profit, organized as a sole proprietorship, corporation, or professional partnership, and fall within the size guidelines set by the SBA.[14] However, the SBA has many tools and resources available to help an early-stage business meet the criteria for a loan, so it is a very good option to at least research. Understand all the terms of the loan before you sign it.

Small-business loans also have useful tax-deduction incentives, but this can be tricky to navigate. Seek multiple perspectives and legal counsel to ensure success.

Pros	Cons
SBA loans can be easier to qualify for than regular bank loans and allow you to make lower payments over a longer period of time.	SBA loans are often risk-averse and can be difficult to navigate and slow to get.
Small-business loans also have useful tax-deduction incentives.	They may require personal guarantees that put your personal assets at risk in case of a default in repayment.

EARLY-STAGE CAPITAL OPTION: Retirement-Fund Financing

Use your existing IRA or 401(k) retirement plan to fund your business.

Many (but not all) 401(k)s have a loan provision. You need to know what the payback requirements are and by when you have to replenish the funds or pay a high penalty. Your fund may also allow you to buy stock should you want to purchase a company within the 401(k). It is imperative to have the right advisors involved to comply with the ERISA and IRS requirements.[15] Make sure they have done what you want to do successfully with other clients. It is important that you really understand the viability of your business and the impact it will have on your life before you bet this asset on your business. Tread very carefully in reviewing this option.

Pros	Cons
You can purchase a business as an investment inside your retirement plan without paying early distribution penalties. If you reinvest, your profits are tax-deferred in your pension.	Must have the right advisors and follow the rules carefully, or you could have unintended tax penalties. More important, if your business fails, your retirement nest egg is gone.

EARLY-STAGE CAPITAL OPTION: Grants

Company grants and contests awarded by government organizations, nonprofits, and/or foundations.

Although there are very few grants offered by the government, there are a number of nonprofit organizations (the Mass Challenge and Make Mine a Million, for example) that have annual competitions for grant money.[16,17] Smaller grants are also appearing specifically targeted to women, such as the Eileen Fischer Foundation's Women-Owned Business Grants, where winning applicants are awarded $10,000.[18]

Pros	Cons
Requires no payback as long as you satisfy the requirements of the grant.	Applying (and competing) for grants is time-consuming, meaning you're spending less time on your business. Grants generally provide only small amounts of investment.

EARLY-STAGE CAPITAL OPTION: Incubators

Programs designed to accelerate the successful inception and evolution of entrepreneurial companies through an array of business-support resources and services.

A number of technology-oriented **incubator** groups act as accelerator centers, offering professional development, networking opportunities, training, consulting, and ongoing support for members.

Examples include TechStars Network[19] (a national incubator group) and angel boot camps. Many college-area communities, such as the Cambridge Innovation Center,[20] provide office-space solutions for growing start-ups and small businesses.

Incubators are also a kind of *angel investment* (more information follows on angel investment in the section on the growth stage). Opportunities vary broadly. Participants are often required to pay a competition fee to be included in an incubator, and incubators may want a piece of your business.

Pros	Cons
Incubators provide office space and initial seed money. They offer mentorship and an infusion of creativity to promising companies, and some put them through entrepreneurial boot camps to get them ready for investment.	Highly competitive with less than 10 percent of applicants gaining admittance to an incubator.

EARLY-STAGE CAPITAL OPTION: Other People's Resources/Money
You share resources through strategic alliances and joint ventures to achieve a common goal.

When two or more entities come together in a temporary partnership it is sometimes termed a **joint venture**, or a **longer-term strategic alliance**. Like any contractual agreement, it is critical that you seek the advice of financial and legal counsel.

Make sure that you and your potential partner are both equally committed and willing to work cooperatively, and that you're willing to allow others to share in the decisions of your business. Understand how the strengths of your potential partner complement your own and establish early on expectations and what both parties are capable of contributing. Be sure you are both committed to focusing on the future of the partnership, rather than just the immediate returns.

Pros	Cons
Usually bring complementary goals and strengths to your business, and share risk, resources, and new opportunities for learning. Very effective for accessing and managing suppliers and distributors of your product or service.	When you take on a joint venture or leverage other people's money and resources, they will also have a say in how you make your business decisions.

EARLY-STAGE CAPITAL OPTION: Local Business-Development Money

In many urban areas, there are business-development organizations in place to encourage local growth.

These loans usually stem from a local community program to offset the impact of an infrastructure change. For example, in Seattle, the development of a light-rail line through the city provided incentive loans to many small businesses affected by the construction. The loans helped them obtain working capital, make equipment purchases, refinance existing debt, and improve or expand their businesses.[21]

There are also stimulus loans, which are awarded to emerging businesses with viable business plans that will have a quick or positive impact on a local community, or to draw a business to relocate to a new community. Stimulus loans help smaller or newer businesses meet credit needs quickly and can range from a $10,000 emerging-entrepreneur loan to $50,000 for businesses willing to relocate to a new area.

Pros	Cons
Qualifications are different than for traditional small-business loans and place more weight on the character, business capacity, and projected cash flow, as well as the impact a business will have on the local community.	Highly competitive, and there are strings attached. Not all communities earmark these types of loans.

Growth Stage

The next stage—**growth capital**—is all about scaling. Typically, the growth-capital space is where entrepreneurs look to take on private equity in the form of venture capital, angel investors, or other private equity firms in order to scale their businesses rapidly. While attracting this kind of capital can be appealing, it should be done with some forethought as to what you want to get out of the arrangement and be supported by careful planning in the start-up and early-stage arrangements you make so that you have room to give only as much of the company away as you feel comfortable.

GROWTH-STAGE CAPITAL OPTION: Angel Investment Groups

Affluent individuals who invest personal capital in exchange for convertible debt or equity.

While **angel investors** are often found initially among an entrepreneur's family and friends, there are a number of more formal angel-investor groups and networks who share research and pool their capital to invest in a company. Recently, a number of women-led angel investment groups and networks have emerged as more formal entities (such as Golden Seeds).[22]

Angels often provide helpful mentoring to entrepreneurs, so look for those who spend time working with entrepreneurs to set milestones and coach them about funding needs.

Many angel investments are lost completely when early-stage companies fail. Because of the risk, angels require a higher return on their investment (be prepared to return them ten times their original investment) and a defined exit strategy such as an initial public offering or acquisition within a relatively short time period.

Although you must be willing to pay better-than-market interest on the loan, it gives you the ability to move into an equity financing arrangement later on by offering to convert that debt for early-stage seed investors at a lower price than the next equity investor.

Pros	Cons
Fill the gap between friends and family loans and venture capital by providing larger amounts of seed money. More personally committed to the success of an individual entrepreneur, and may bring seasoned advisors as well as investors into your business.	Because they are focused on the individual, there tends to be a long courting process involved before an angel group will take you on board.

GROWTH-STAGE CAPITAL OPTION: Venture Funding

A group or entity takes a large stake in your business.

Unlike angels, **venture-capital (VC) groups** are not investing personal capital but rather capital that stems from a fund or investment portfolio.

However, they do share the same objective as an angel in that their goal is to exponentially grow a company. They often provide the expertise or resources the entrepreneur is lacking (such as legal advice, technology development, or marketing knowledge) and the money needed to increase a company's infrastructure quickly to grow and scale rapidly.

Like angel-investment groups, VCs require higher interest rates and a specifically defined exit strategy. It is important to remember that VCs are usually focused first on the exponential growth on their investment. The impact is that what you believe needs to happen for your business may be secondary to their investment.

Pros	Cons
Access to larger amounts of capital necessary to scale and expand a business quickly.	Very focused on payout and exit strategy, which can be difficult to manage. Limits your potential upside profit. If the venture capitalist(VC) takes a large stake in your business, he or she may see the profits before you do.

GROWTH-STAGE CAPITAL OPTION: Private Equity Groups

Take a private equity stake in small- and middle-market companies looking to drive steady growth and profitability.

Private equity partners often take on a senior management or board-level role to ensure control and growth, so it is important to be clear about the terms, scope, and time frame.

While you have your goals, private equity groups have their own set of goals, preferences, investment strategies, and terms to eliminate as much of the risk for them as possible before going into the deal.

Although they can provide an entrepreneur with the "golden egg" needed to nurture expansion or fulfill your product development plan, they may bring in new officers to your company, and it is important that they are fully aligned with your vision, or it can significantly reduce the control you have over your company's future.

Pros	Cons
Provide seasoned expertise and talent. Infuse stability and capital into business to direct refinancing or new assets. Get your company ready for acquisition or buyout.	They take a majority stake and control over you *and* your business.

The SmartGirls Way does not endorse or recommend any particular funding option over another. In all cases, you need to understand the pros and cons of your funding options and be clear about expectations on both sides.

	Option	Pros	Cons
Stages of Capital: Start-Up	Bootstrapping	Maintain control of business without debt	Must split time between new business and existing job Risk to personal financial situation
	Loans from friends and family	Favorable terms Flexible	May give lenders control over your business May jeopardize relationships with friends/family
	Crowd-funding	Payments dependent on success Maintain full control of business	Must have compelling cause or offering Generally more effective for raising money for social causes
	Sweat equity	Provides support and resources to get business off the ground	Talent may put paying work ahead of your needs Talent needs may change over the years Talent may depart

	Option	Pros	Cons
Stages of Capital: Early Stage	Personal loans	Larger loans Terms and expectations are clear and straightforward	Difficult to secure Risk of default or bankruptcy
	Peer-to-peer and micro-lending	No middleman Potential for further investment	Smaller amounts of money More time and risk for investors May be governed by securities laws
	Small Business Administration loans	Easier to qualify for Lower payments and longer repayment period Tax incentives	Risk-averse Difficult to navigate Slow process May require personal guarantees (risk of default)
	Retirement fund financing	No early distribution penalties Reinvested profits are tax-deferred	Must have the right advisors Risk losing retirement nest egg
	Grants	Requires no payback	Process is time-consuming Generally small amounts
	Incubators	Office space and seed money provided Offer mentorship and infusion of creativity Entrepreneurial "boot camp"	Highly competitive
	Other people's resources/money	Brings complementary goals and strengths Effective for accessing and managing supply chain	May give lenders control over your business
	Local business development money	Qualify based on character, business capacity, projected cash flow, and community impact	Highly competitive Strings attached Not available in all communities

	Option	Pros	Cons
Stages of Capital: Growth Stage	Angel investment groups	Larger amounts of seed money than family/friends loans More personally committed to success May bring seasoned advisors	Long courting process
	Venture funding	Larger amounts of capital	Very focused on payout and exit strategy Limits potential upside profit VC may see profits before you do
	Private equity groups	Provide seasoned expertise and talent Infuse stability and capital Get company ready for acquisition or buyout	Take a majority stake and control over you and your business

While it is important to fund your business, it is equally important to keep it sovereign so that you have the flexibility and control over future decisions. Many of the forms of finance available today are all about attachment and laying claim to your business. Your investors will want ultimate protection, but you should never agree to terms you can't live with.

CREATIVITY, INTEGRITY, & WEAVING

Underwriting yourself requires Creativity, Integrity, and Weaving skills. You will have to get creative to find multilevel financial platforms that best suit your needs, and you will need to act with Integrity in all of those interactions. Weaving is probably one of the most important strengths in the bankrolling process because of the networking and connections you will need to make to meet investors and then nurture and grow those relationships to the point where they feel confident investing in you.

Start!

You've drafted your value proposition, organized and committed to your first move, and created a business plan to underwrite yourself. The last step in the FOCUS stage is to *start!*

To help you do this, we've shared some SmartGirls Way examples and behaviors that you can use immediately.

Identify Your First "Quick Wins"

It is very rare that any entrepreneur becomes an overnight success. When you start implementing your business plan, reaching your long-term objectives may seem a distant goal. You can keep your energy and your business moving along by asking yourself, "What are my **quick wins**?"

After developing her product team and building AllVoices, Amra Tareen needed to attract additional financing in order to scale to the next stage of her business plan. Her first quick win was to quickly grow her writer base.

Amra set specific metrics in order to attract readers. Her team created different news pages with specific angles and drove traffic to those pages via social-media outreach. She used search-engine marketing to ensure that people searching by topic could find AllVoices news. They measured each campaign weekly with a focus of spreading the word and getting people to register and start writing, keeping only the best campaigns. She kept iterating her campaigns, but the metrics by which she measured her success—driving traffic to the site to support her advertising revenue model—remained the same.

While word of mouth and encouraging people to contribute to the site was Amra's strategy, it was really the communication of her vision that drove registration and early growth. "When your vision becomes something everyone else can relate to, it grows. AllVoices was the platform where people were able to share what really mattered," she says.

Which is why during the heart of the economic crisis in 2009, Amra was able to secure more funding.

"Even though news itself is a perishable commodity and people don't want to fund news sites, our growth was different. The same investor originally invested $4.5 million and then a total of $9 million because he saw the tremendous growth and response to what people were writing and reading compared to other websites," she says.

A little over two years after its launch, AllVoices was receiving 11 million unique readers a month reading user-generated content created by 440,000 writers from 180 countries.

By setting out to define what *success looks like today in the context of your larger goal,* you create feasible accomplishments from day to day. What gets measured gets done, so setting out weekly and monthly goals against these initial quick-win activities will keep you moving in the right direction.

Solicit Feedback, Listen to It, and Use It Immediately

When you begin to bring your business out in the world, you will invariably receive feedback from others. Some of it will be helpful, and some of it may be frustrating. If you solicit feedback in an objective and focused way, it can help you discern and *hear* the feedback that is most useful and important.

After creating her Devine Delicate paint line, Gretchen Schauffler discovered that customers needed an easier way to sample her custom paint colors than the traditional paint-chip sample, which didn't really provide a true impression of how her colors would look on walls. She also knew that people didn't want to go to the expense—and waste—of testing colors from the traditional quart-sized paint sample. So she landed on the idea of the "Mini Paint Pouch," a two-ounce sample, and began to research how she could create her own sample along with the bags and covers to put them in. The original mock-up was a household plastic freezer bag with sticker label that Gretchen designed herself. When she solicited input from her clients, she knew she was on to a true innovation.

"My customer feedback was consistently that it was a genius idea—and only a woman could have thought of it! Here are the many reasons they gave: You can toss (the pouches) in a purse and not have to worry about them; you can carry ten color samples in one hand; they are fun to squeeze, play with; they are resealable; they do not waste paint, time, or money."

By listening to customer feedback, the Mini Paint Pouch revolutionized the paint industry and changed the way large companies market and sample color to women today.

Maybe you need to do some additional research into the behaviors and buying habits of your customers. Create a simple market survey on Zoomerang or your own website. It is important to create formal listening channels to your customers and stakeholders. Create in-store feedback cards. Solicit feedback on your company Facebook page or create a place on your webpage for customer comments. Respond in a timely manner, thank people for their comments, and let them know their feedback is taken seriously.

Talk It Up

When you are first trying to establish your business, it helps to host some kind of launch event that announces you to the world and gives people a chance to interact with you.

Finding a way to frequently, appropriately, and effectively communicate news and updates about your product and company is one of the best ways to gain support and customers for your business.

> *Create a space and rituals for applying love and energy to your business.*

To keep up the energy and momentum for your business, it is important that you carve out time to build a culture that allows others to share in your purpose and vision for your company. You can do this by consciously infusing Integrity, Creativity, and Passion into everything you do.

For Sheryl O'Loughlin, cofounder of Nest Collective, this idea manifested itself in the form of a culture meeting. From the outset, her team embraced the metaphorical meaning of the company's name, referring to themselves as a flock and adopting individual bird names. "Creating our culture twig by twig was a very deliberate action," she says. "We were creating something good for the world, and when we talked about our purpose, the team really loved and lived the Nest brand and vision."

Every second week, the "flock" would have breakfast at an "all flow" meeting and then discuss the culture they were building together. Team members who worked remotely from the office would attend by video conference. Meetings would often begin with members calling off their bird names. The meeting was an intentional ritual for creating "pause" in the day-to-day business to stop and think about the big picture, which can be a challenge at times for fast-growing companies.

Sheryl tied this back to another organic metaphor: "We talked about the rings of a tree, and we understood that we were the center rings and that the actions we took were going to influence the eventual shape of that tree."

Owners of women-led businesses make a conscious decision to nurture and create supportive space. It's not just about creating an encouraging work environment; it's about creating a greater return on your investment. Research on women in development indicates that the returns on investment in women are much higher than for men. Women are more likely to share their gains in education, health, and resources with members of their families and their communities at large. Research on microfinance indicates that the same is true for economic investments. Women are simply more likely to work for, buy for, and share their economic and noneconomic rewards with other people.[23]

When you create a culture that includes positive rituals and recognition for your team and supporters, you will help your team—and you—become more confident in your skills and more alert to the existence of untapped opportunities.

Celebrate!

There will be times when you're working so hard that you forget to stop and acknowledge your efforts and accomplishments. This can be detrimental to the culture and vitality of your business. You have built a network of support with your Champions, Cheerleaders, and Caretakers. Make sure you take the time to celebrate your success and efforts with all of them.

PASSION, CURIOSITY, & WEAVING

Passion, Curiosity, and Weaving will also play critical roles in Start! Your Passion is the spark that ignites your first quick win and will be apparent when you are talking up your business to others. When you solicit feedback, Curiosity will help you listen for insights and push you toward new solutions. Together, they will optimize your ability to Weave the ideas and information you receive into the actions, rituals, and activities that drive your early days as an entrepreneur.

7

THRIVE

The third and final stage of the SmartGirls Methodology is scaling your business to THRIVE.

As we mentioned earlier in this book, entrepreneurism has a terrible reputation as a death wish, a disease, or at the very least, the breeding ground for an unhealthy lifestyle. We disagree. That was the old entrepreneurism—a pre-recession way of looking at business. The SmartGirls Way definition is different.

We believe that entrepreneurs take responsibility to make their great ideas happen in the context of a complete life—aligning business goals with family and community, and fitting business into a worldview for a healthy and thriving planet. Entrepreneurs can be wildly successful; we believe many of you will exceed your greatest expectations for financial success. But the entrepreneurial life needs to be one that is in balance. If you can achieve balance in work, you, your business, your family, and our world will THRIVE!

While the first two stages of the SmartGirls Methodology are focused on activities and behaviors necessary for success in designing and launching your business, THRIVE is focused on *five core principles* critical to scaling and operating successful business.

THRIVE stands for Trust, Honesty, Responsibility, Intention, Values, and Empowerment.

Trust

Trust is the first of the THRIVE principles, and it begins with the trust you must have in yourself and your dream. Your trust in yourself will be directly related to your self-confidence and therefore the confidence that your customers, employees, investors, and suppliers will place in you. This trust and confidence is not dependent upon how you feel in the moment—at some point, we all experience fear, uncertainty, and doubt. A bad day or fearful moment does not have to damage your trust in yourself or the confidence that others place in you. Trust is dependent on how you act in the moment.

In terms of actions and behaviors, the most important SmartGirls Way characteristic for building trust is Integrity. You build trust with every encounter—delivering a product or service to a client or customer on time, paying your suppliers in a timely manner, and providing great customer service.

Take a moment and think about your interactions with those you encounter every day. Here are a few Integrity questions that can help you reflect on your interactions.

> When I am trusting my own judgment, have I put Intuition in balance with Curiosity and Weaving by considering others' inputs and needs?

> Can I listen without judging when someone has an opinion about a decision I need to make?

> Am I able to negotiate and make good agreements—ones that I am happy to hold myself to and feel confident that I can deliver on?

If you can answer these positively, it will help you strengthen your ability to create trust and build confidence.

Trust is dependent upon the credibility of past experiences. When your actions are aligned with your Integrity, you create an "emotional bank account" of credibility. These past interactions become an asset when a problem arises, and they are one of three cornerstones in building your Trust Triangle.

The Trust Triangle

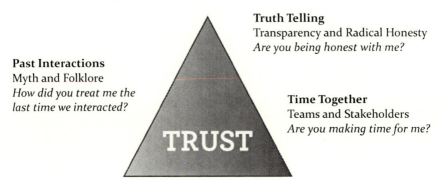

You draw upon the *Past Interactions* asset during a crisis. It is the interaction during an emergency or an emotionally heightened situation that people most remember. Your *actions* during these encounters are critical because no matter how the situation was resolved, what people most remember is how the people they are counting on treat them.

The second cornerstone of the Trust Triangle is *Time Together,* and it is an absolute nonnegotiable in terms of building authentic, trusting relationships. Time Together can range from minutes to hours spent with employees and suppliers, but no matter whom you encounter, you need to demonstrate that you value people's time and needs. Generally, the more required from the relationship—in other words, those contracts that are interdependent as well as contractual—the more time they require to create and maintain trust.

For entrepreneurs, the rapid pace of growth and business often makes this the hardest component of the Trust Triangle, because time is usually the biggest hurdle. You can't be everywhere at once, so it is important to set up regular communication rituals and systems with all of your stakeholders. This may take the form of regular customer-feedback sessions, weekly or daily staff meetings, a quarterly advisory-board meeting, and most important, individual interactions like your first and last phone call of the day. When your communications actions are consistent, people know when they can expect to hear from you, and you foster comfort and productivity in the form of routine.

A word of caution: It is important to remember that Time Together is an in-person effort. It's tempting to rely upon email for communicating, but that can be detrimental to trust building if you use it to convey personal feedback—it is too easy for people to misinterpret the tone and context of email missives. To build a personal rapport, you must also communicate in person. This is especially important if you work within a distance-based team, so find ways to meet key stakeholders face-to-face.

Make the time to create positive interactions, be open and straightforward, be consistent and reliable, and spend the appropriate amount of time to maintain your relationships. The trust you build will quickly become a key differentiator in the success of your business and your life.

The pinnacle of your Trust Triangle is *Truth Telling,* and we will discuss this aspect more in the next section, dedicated to Honesty. In the meantime, the most important question to ask yourself to ensure that you are effectively and consistently delivering on the principle of trust is this:

Can people count on me to do, say, and deliver what I say I will?

INTEGRITY & INTUITION

Your strength in building trust comes from Integrity and Intuition. When you continuously represent yourself, your company, and your brand with Integrity, people know that they can rely on your word and know what you can be counted on to deliver. When you tap your Intuition, you don't ignore or shy away from conflicts, and you follow your instincts about when and how to communicate.

Honesty

Most people believe they are honest. Most people also tell at least the occasional "little white lie," and we're not trying to suggest that the only way through life is without exaggeration. However, basic honesty and transparency are critical to your success, and as the Trust Triangle above represents, it goes beyond the ability to tell the truth with a willingness to give people all the information they need. Withholding important information is the same as not telling the truth.

How we tell the truth is just as important. A common myth is that women must adopt aggressive "alpha-male" behaviors to succeed in business. The truth behind this is that passivity in how women act and communicate in business can negatively impact their success. The culprit here is the distinction between agreeableness and honesty.[1] To be truly transparent, you need to embrace a kind of honesty that can be blunt when necessary. When we fail to be direct in our actions and communications, we negatively impact the success of our business. This is particularly important if women are to be taken seriously as entrepreneurs.

Here are some examples when **radical honesty** can be required:

› You are meeting with a potential investor or sponsor and notice that a good deal of attention is being paid to how you look instead of what you are saying.

› You are discussing implementation and operations with an acquaintance who seems much more interested in your business model than he or she has in the past—you begin to wonder if you are in fact talking to a future competitor.
› For the third or fourth time, you are having the same performance discussion with a supplier or employee who does not take you seriously.

In these situations and many others, you must have the courage for radical honesty. Put the entire truth—what you see, what you sense, and the questions you have—on the table in a direct and no-nonsense way. Sexism is still a reality in our world, but it doesn't have to become a barrier to your success. Nor does it mean you have to offend or alienate while making your point. We've found that speaking the truth in a calm, non-judging, but not-to-be-ignored fashion can make all the difference.

When it comes to honesty, consistency matters. You can't play along and flirt one week and then demand businesslike attention the next. The same can be said with passive behavior. If you don't stand up and address an issue when it arises, you can't expect people to change their behavior, nor can you be surprised when that behavior continues. Inconsistency in how you engage and represent yourself just adds to the confusion.

The SmartGirls Mirror characteristic Intuition plays a critical role in honesty. When you stop and intuitively assess a situation, you focus on the deep honesty embedded in that situation. In Chapter 3, we discussed the importance of phrasing in addressing conflict situations that require deep honesty, as well as a woman's tendency to choose feeling words that convey emotion instead of feeling words that convey data.

Given the above situations, here are some potential *radically honest responses*—of course, you can think of others as well, and we'd love to hear how you've handled similar situations. The goal is to address and defuse the situation with an honest and calm response while maintaining or improving the relationship.

Situation: You are meeting with a potential investor or sponsor and notice that a good deal of attention is being paid to how you look instead of to what you are saying.

"I can't help but notice that you seem distracted. Is there something you need to tell me? This is a really important topic and critical to my business. I'm happy to reschedule to a time that works better for you if you like."

The deep honesty in the example above is that you let that person know that you are aware he is not paying attention, and that you are interested in talking business. Not getting flustered or calling it "flirting" tells him you are harder to rattle than he thinks.

Situation: You are discussing implementation and operations with an acquaintance who seems much more interested in your business model than he or she has in the past—you begin to wonder if you are talking to a future competitor.

"I notice that you are really interested in details today in a way you haven't been before. This conversation is making me feel a little uncomfortable about that, considering the sensitivity of this information. Can you tell me about why you are so interested?"

The deep honesty in this situation is acknowledging that you have noticed the change in interest and that your Intuition is guiding you to be cautious. In this situation, don't hesitate to ask for an NDA.

Situation: For the third or fourth time, you are having the same performance discussion with a supplier who does not take you seriously.

"I really like your product, but this issue is a serious one for my business. Can you tell me what you think we should do to fix this situation? If we cannot resolve it to my satisfaction today, I'll have to find another source or a substitute."

The deep honesty in this situation is that you have clearly stated with some clarity the parameters for continued engagement, and you've opened the door for an honest dialogue.

A Word About Bragging

Finally, a word about bragging: Don't be shy about sharing your successes. As girls, we're taught to be modest about our accomplishments. As adults, we read articles about how to make sure male colleagues don't feel bad when we take credit for our successes. The consensus? It's a risky business for women to crow even when the bragging rights are well-deserved.

For women entrepreneurs, this lack of bragging is often construed as a lack of confidence in themselves or their business. So how does bragging relate to honesty?

> *Honest* self-acknowledgment about your accomplishments and your personal brilliance is the key to walking into a room filled with self-confidence!

Here are four behaviors you can immediately and regularly practice to create radically honest confidence.

1. Every week, find something that you or one of your staff members did that was creative, courageous, and/or smart, and communicate it to the people who are important to your business. Don't overdo it—just be authentic and appropriately proud.

2. When you face a challenge, stop and *listen* to what your Intuition is telling you and *be present* with your reaction and the reactions of others. Don't judge or be judged by it. Just note it and note how you feel about it.

3. Be aware of passive-aggressive behavior, both yours and others'. When you notice something is going on, address it in a calm and straightforward manner.

4. When you're wrong or you make a mistake, be honest and say so. We often learn more from our mistakes than we do from our successes. Finding the lesson in every situation is part of building wisdom. And from wisdom stems confidence and an ability to be authentically honest and self-aware.

> **INTEGRITY & INTUITION**
>
> *When we leverage our Integrity and Intuition, we find our way to deep honesty and are able to present ourselves in a more confident and direct manner in difficult situations.*

Responsibility

Responsibility for an entrepreneur means *you are your business*. Everything your business does is your responsibility. In fact, our definition of "entrepreneur" is a woman who is willing to accept responsibility and accountability for her ViBI and create a business, a social enterprise, or a breakthrough project around it.

Responsibility is ownership. As an owner, it's critical for you to have a strong understanding of what ownership means to you and *how you will share that responsibility and accountability with others*. Creating clarity and control is critical for *effectively* engaging with partners, investors, employees, and customers the SmartGirls Way. There are a few simple—but critical—success factors to consider:

First, in matters of control, you need to *determine who is accountable for what*. To put a finer point on it, as an entrepreneur, even if you put someone else in charge of something, you are ultimately accountable for the outcome.

Second, *clarity of control can come only through clear, consistent, and what feels like constant communication*. The reality of entrepreneurship means that things are constantly in motion, and if it's going well, you and your team will be moving very rapidly. The initial idea you come up with will probably not be the final idea you implement. This is simply evolution, and it can be very powerful. After all, the best products and services respond to the market and improve. However, this nimbleness and flexibility also requires shifts in direction and responsibility that have to be clearly defined and communicated to your team.

Finally, as you grow and scale your business, you need to *create a process for achieving clarity of control*. A **RASI chart** (which stands for Responsibility, Accountability, Support, and Inform) is one of the most common tools used for this purpose. Create your own RASI chart like the one below and keep it updated and in the hands of your team.

RASI Chart Example

	Responsibility	Accountability	Support	Inform
Definition	The person whose job it is to get a particular project, task, or process done. The person in control of the project and the outcome.	The person who will ultimately "hold the bag" on outcomes; often but not always the responsible party.	People clearly identified to support the person who is responsible. Team members, support personnel, vendors, etc.	People who must be kept in the loop about the project/assignment. This usually includes the person accountable and other team members impacted by the activity.
Person 1		X		X
Person 2	X			
Person 3			X	X

Responsibility drives you and your team to do your best. If you set a high standard and create clear expectations around responsibility from the beginning, your team will thrive. Learning from mistakes while accepting responsibility not only makes things "right," it helps others to grow, too.

Finally, responsibility is important for another reason. As more people take responsibility and accountability for the impact a business has on society, the greater the benefit to people and the planet.

CURIOSITY & CREATIVITY

Curiosity and Creativity are helpful strengths in creating clarity and control. When we seek solutions and enlist others to help us, we organize and motivate our teams to engage in a responsible way. An entrepreneur's passion does much to instill accountability because it is the passion and commitment to your ViBI that drives you—and others—to work hard and take ownership of the outcomes of your work.

Intention

Intention for an entrepreneur and your business is integral to your life. For you to thrive, financially, physically, emotionally, and spiritually, you need to engage with your ViBI in an intentional and committed way every day.

Purposeful engagement with your ViBI and your goals and desires for your overall life is the practice of intention. As an example of this, we discussed in the foreword of this book women entrepreneurs being a critical catalyst for building a vibrant and thriving future—the basis for the next economy and a sustainable planet.

We have also shared examples of businesses that women have started out of an intention to meet a specific unmet need in their lives or communities. When we design an intention that is inclusive of our vision and our families, as well as our inner artist, traveler, and all of the other wonderful ways in which we define our inner selves, we toss the rock that becomes the seed in the pond that becomes the wave of our business.

> *The creation of SmartGirls Way was the logical outgrowth of Jean's lifelong intention—to create constellations of communities for a positive shift on the planet now.*

Clear intention practiced daily will guide you to correct action. As the leader of your company, it can be all too easy to get distracted and lose sight of your intention. This is most true when your business really begins to take off, but it's true even for women who have successfully been running multimillion-dollar businesses for years. As your business grows, there will be new people and new distractions involved. The key to recognizing the difference between a *distraction* and a *redirect*—something that *should* demand your attention—is intention.

There are many resources out there for creating and using intention. We highly recommend you engage in this process if you have not yet done so. If you are already working with intentions, good for you; please remember to keep them active in your life every day.

To get started now, here are a few basics:

› Intentions are formed as questions.
› Intentions are specific.

› Intentions are genuine and come from a place of Integrity.
› Intentions are action-oriented.

For example, our intention for creating the book is

To create a deeply useful and engaging book that will empower, encourage, and embolden women entrepreneurs through a focus on their unique and considerable strengths and by providing practical, usable guidance.

INTEGRITY & PASSION

It should come as no surprise that the strengths that most drive intention are Integrity and Passion. As your business grows, there will be distractions. Maintaining a hold on your Passion can keep you energized through change and growing pains. Integrity will act as your magnet, keeping you on course as your business evolves.

Values

Values are the manifestations of your intentions for your business. At various times as you build your business, you will have to rely on your personal values to guide your choices. As you scale your company, a clearly articulated and purposely created version of your values will guide you and all of those engaged in your company. The most powerful way to engage with your values is by consciously and proactively exploring and articulating your values well ahead of a crisis.

When we introduced Integrity in Chapter 3, we discussed our experience that women most often thrive in businesses that align with their personal sense of Integrity. Your Integrity is a combination of things that ultimately make up your personal code or compass. Integrity causes you to ask questions such as,

Is my business adding value to my life?
my family? my community? the world?

Values are your personal beliefs, principles, and standards of behavior. Your Integrity is made up of your personal values plus preferences that shape your values into beliefs. Values have an emotional component, and therefore we each prioritize our values—whether consciously or not—depending on how strongly we feel about things.

This important element is what makes society so very interesting. While many (if not most) mentally and emotionally healthy people have a number of common values, their feelings about the relative importance of these values vary wildly. That makes for the most amazing and enlightening conversations; these strong beliefs and feelings are typically backed by our life experiences.

The power of understanding your personal values is not just the ability to articulate them to your team, but to better understand the experiences and prejudices that have led you to your current value set.

Entrepreneurs are constantly challenged through new ideas, data, and opportunities. Knowing how your values are affecting your choices and decisions can save you from mistakes and increase your ability to reflectively and effectively listen to—and learn from—others.

Defining their personal values was one of the first things Africa Direct founders Elizabeth Bennett and Sara Luther did for their business. After receiving advice about their mission and concept that they felt could endanger the viability of their business (such as being asked to lie on customs forms), the couple sat down and defined four operating principles that have lasted throughout their sixteen years in business. They are:

1. Take risks, but don't bet the farm.

2. Do well by doing good.

3. Be honest and legal.

4. Be customer-centric.

"It was important for us to understand the ramifications of the people and business decisions we had to make—good, neutral, or otherwise. When you do this, you begin to realize your power in the decisions you have," Elizabeth explains.

To help you focus on your personal values, following is an extensive (but not exhaustive) list of personal values. Circle the values most important to you, or come up with your own and write them on the blanks provided.

Exercise 3: Defining Your Values

Accomplishment	Fun	Security
Accountability	Global awareness/ worldview	Selflessness (giving of self to others)
Accuracy		
Acknowledgment	Hard work	Self-reliance
Adventure	Honesty	Simplicity
Beauty	Improvement	Skill
Calm, peacefulness	Independence	Spirituality
Challenge	Individuality	Stability
Change	Innovation	Status
Collaboration	Justice/Merit	Strength, will
Commitment	Kindness	Teamwork
Community	Leadership	Timeliness
Compassion	Loyalty	Tolerance
Competence	Openness	Tradition
Competition	Patriotism	Tranquility
Connection	Peace	Trust
Democracy	Perfection	Truth
Discipline	Personal growth	Unity
Discovery	Power	Variety
Efficiency	Progress	Wisdom
Equality	Prosperity	_____
Fairness	Reliability	
Faith	Resourcefulness	_____
Family	Respect	
Freedom	Responsiveness	_____
Friendship	Safety	

Then, spend some time thinking about how you would answer this question:

What values would you give up if forced to?

Is that too hard? Try this exercise:

Exercise 4: Prioritizing Your Values

You're being chased through a jungle by a tiger, and your values are in a bag on your back. You have to lighten your load. You're forced to choose.

> Which values remain in the bag the longest, and why?
>
> How do these values help your business?
>
> Where do they show up in your life every day?
>
> How might your values be limiting your experience?

Keep these values handy. They form the basis of your Integrity and will guide you to success.

> **INTEGRITY**
>
> *Integrity is the key driver of your values. Your values will have meaning for you, but how you convey those values, in intention and behavior, will determine how aligned your values are with your business.*

Empowerment

Empowerment is the last and perhaps most important principle, because to THRIVE, you must empower yourself, your dreams, your team, and others.

The kind of empowerment that we are talking about is the modern definition: *making others stronger and more confident in claiming their rights and managing their lives.* As entrepreneurs, we empower ourselves and our ViBI. As you grow your business, there is another definition that can give specific insight into the empowerment that entrepreneurs need to bring to bear for themselves and for others. That definition is to *qualify*. To qualify means to become eligible—it is earned. Continuing to earn your empowerment requires two things.

First, you will need to qualify yourself by:

› Ensuring that you remain connected to and energized by your ViBI

- Finding ways to continuously learn and be challenged
- Finding mentors and role models to help you navigate the waters
- Connecting to communities that encourage and inspire you

Second, you can qualify your team by:

- Finding good fits—hiring and engaging team members who augment and balance your strengths
- Creating clear expectations, accountability, and deliverables
- Providing the right resources, background, and insight for success
- Acknowledging and rewarding your team
- Providing training and hands-on time
- Communicate. Communicate. Communicate!

If your team members are joining you in a start-up, they should be clear about the pace, fluidity, and risk. Nothing works better than genuine acknowledgment of those aspects. It is very important that you provide one-on-one time with your staff; employees need to spend time with you. No matter how quickly you grow or how big you get, if you want people to understand your values, they need to get a glimpse inside your head and learn the reasons that motivated you to launch your ViBI in the first place.

More than anything else, you are the chief *communication* officer for your company. The role of CEO communication is critical, but never more so than in a start-up.

There are entire books written on how to be an effective communicator. If you are not comfortable with being the face of your company, we highly encourage you to get some personal coaching on your presentation and communications skills. However, when it comes to communication with your internal and external audiences, there are essentially three basic rules to remember:

1. **Be truthful and honest in all of your communications.**
    If you don't know something, say so. You will not always have all the answers. If you come across an issue or a request that you can't answer, don't bluff your way through it; people will see through it at great cost to your credibility.

An honest response—"I don't know the answer to that question, but I will look into it and get back to you."—is always appropriate. Then, make sure you do exactly that.

2. **Choose appropriate communications tools for appropriate information.**
We talked earlier in this chapter about the dangers of electronic communications. Don't convey bad news or negative feedback in an email. Take the personal responsibility to intentionally sit down and directly address challenges and issues with people, and they will soon learn to do the same with you.

Carefully consider the appropriate vehicles for conveying information. Before Tweeting about a new business deal, make sure it is appropriate. Use blogs and Facebook pages to appropriately engage with customers, and make sure you also respond and listen to their feedback.

3. **Communicate in person and often with employees, investors, and customers.**
In most cases, failure to mobilize a team for change can be attributed to poor communication, and the same can be said when you're trying to promote your brand. Your Passion and Integrity are best conveyed in person.[2]

Every communication you have is a representation of you *and* your brand. If you ardently adhere to the trust, honesty, responsibility, intention, values, and empowerment principles of THRIVE, you have the foundation of good communication.

CURIOSITY, PASSION, & WEAVING

Curiosity, Weaving, and Passion are key amplifiers of empowerment. When you remain curious, you encourage and "qualify" yourself and others to be open. When you weave, you help yourself and others make the necessary connections to connect and inspire. When your Passion comes across in your communications, you create an open and honest environment for growth.

8

Not-So-Final Words

It's often hard to know how to wrap up. There's no dramatic ending or a post-drama dénouement here. The stories we have told are not over—far from it. In most cases, they are just beginning. Your story is also being written right now—as you read the book, complete the exercises, talk to friends and family about your ViBI or your business, and create the intention to build the muscle for your *success*. Your story will evolve and continue as you create your network and partnerships for scaling or selling your business and preparing for your next big thing.

What this chapter *is* about is the bridge to your next adventure, your insights, and your stories. We hope that many of them will be in our next book—or *your* first book about your own business.

What we've included here are key things we've learned about that bridge and what is required to get from one side to the other. Picture one of those swinging, rain-forest footbridges—super-scary, but *so* exciting when you are on the other side. There is no doubt entrepreneurs must cross this bridge, sometimes more than once, and often when they least expect it. But they do it. We did it. And so will you.

Skills for Successful Bridge Crossing

First—**keep your eye on the other side**. You have built a clear vision of your business from your original inspiration. Keep your ViBI in your heart and on your lips. Why?

Guess what happens when you look down.
You see the *fall,* not the *goal.*

We've come to understand that it is not a fear of failure that most often keeps women from accessing their deepest truths and following their greatest dreams. It's a fear of *falling*—of not having a safety net and not knowing how they would feel, even about themselves, if they fall.

But so what?

Honestly and straightforwardly think about the worst-case scenario. Jean hates to do that, but she and her husband sail. The only thing worse than having something bad happen on a sailboat is not being prepared when something bad happens on a sailboat. So she doesn't dwell on it, but she understands what the options are if the worst should happen. Do the same for your entrepreneurial adventures. Once you look at that scenario, put it away and keep your eye on the other side of the bridge. You know you will be fine even if you fall.

>Motto: **Keep your eye on the prize.** Every day. All the time. Especially when you're tempted to look down!

Second—**Be strong**. It's hard to have the energy to stride confidently across the bridge if you are tired, sick, or generally road-weary. This is tough for women entrepreneurs. We have not yet met the woman entrepreneur, with or without a family, who is not the heart and soul of her personal community. Like we said, it's our nature to nurture, and we want to do it.

However, you are no good to anyone if you are run-down. It can lead to discouragement and false choices. The long view is this—if you are following your dream, you are going to be better for yourself, your family, your community, and the world. But you want to *be* there at the end to enjoy it as well.

Simply put, physical and emotional self-care is critical. It can be hard to eat right, exercise, get enough sleep, and de-stress.

Focus on four simple things:

> **Eat healthy**. This means whole and nutritious food. Have healthy food around that you can eat when you're hungry, because of course, you skip regular meals. Many small meals are better than a few large ones.

> **Drink water**. There's no debate on this in the medical community—most of us do not drink enough water. Water provides multiple benefits and is the key to so many things, including balancing energy. Plus, there is something interestingly calming about just stopping and drinking a glass of water.

Move. Whether it is a focused and energetic walk, run, bike ride with the kids, or dancing to your favorite music, move. It doesn't have to be an activity that you plan for hours and diverts your attention for hours. Beyond the long-term health benefits, you will also feel better in the moment, gain insights and perspective, and get a much-deserved mental break.

Sleep. It's ironic for us to be telling you this—Jean is a lifetime insomniac, and Tracey has three young children. But we do it. We get as much sleep as we can. The toll on the body caused by persistent sleep deprivation is well-known. What's not as well-known is that you can play it on the edge for a pretty long time and start to believe that you have cheated fate. But then you get sick—which requires you to go to bed to sleep. And if you can nap, do that too. Lots of great ideas and connections are made while we are sleeping.

> Motto: **Remember that you are your own best asset.**
> Taking care of yourself *and* your business is critical.

Third—**Make sure the rooting section is ready!** By now, you know how important we believe your personal support system is to your success, and you've put serious thought into the makeup of your own support system—your personal safety net. It's a critical part of the entrepreneurial ecosystem for women, not well-documented in general entrepreneurial terms, yet critical to success. If you've realized your support system is weak or lacking definition and structure, fix that *now*.

It's not easy, but take it from us, it can be a powerful and life-changing conversation. It doesn't have to be about your being selfish, or your husband and family or other significant people in your life indulging you while you pursue your dream. It can be the most amazing window to partnership and the greatest boon to your relationships that you will ever have. But there are a few tricks to getting and *keeping* the commitments clear and the partnership healthy.

› Assume that *your* happiness and fulfillment are important to your partner, friends, and family, and that *they care*.

› Make sure that you are clear about what you need and how they can help.

- Keep your side of the commitment.
- Clarify that this is a covenant, not a contract.
- Be specific and keep the conversation dynamic and alive.

> Motto: **It takes a village.** What's true for child-rearing is also true for growing a business. Engage your community of supporters early and often.

New Habits

As you engage with your ViBI and build your business, you begin to have an entirely new language. No matter your past experience, every new business has its own idiom, culture, and energy. This language will be very exciting to you—even more so because you will be learning so much on a daily basis.

Along with this new language, you are also evolving as a person. It's true for all of us that as we grow and learn, we understand more not only about the world but about ourselves. When you engage in large efforts that are as creative, demanding, and personal as building your own business, this evolution is accelerated.

Your rapidly changing world and the high energy it generates can sometimes be overwhelming to others. Those closest to you—your family and your "safety-net" people—will have enough information about what is driving you that they will likely get caught up in the excitement as well, helping them be part of your story and keeping them "in the camp."

For other people in your life—the friends you don't see on a regular basis or those who are activity- or opportunity-specific—you may need a different strategy. They may not know what you are up to, what's exciting you, or why you are not more available. You may have to dramatically change your schedule to build your business. You may be preoccupied and interested mostly (or even only) in your business. This is perfectly natural. While your business may be the biggest thing you will ever do in your life, you may find it difficult for the other women in your life to relate.

You don't have to lose your friends to build your business, but you may have to engage some special communications or strategies.

The most important thing you can do is invite people to help you improve what you are doing. Be open and accept their input. Don't try to correct them if they don't know what they're talking about. Point them to your materials and website and ask for their comments.

And be prepared to decide whether you want to continue some friendships. Not every friend will appreciate the new skin you are growing. You will have confidence, connections, insights, and power that you've never had before. How that fits for others in your life is not just up to them, it's also up to you. Every person in our lives is part of an amazingly important tapestry that defines who we are and what we have stood for. Some parts of the tapestry are core to the weaving—it doesn't hold together without them. Some are more ornamental or captured in a part of the tapestry that relates to a specific place and time.

The important thing is to be intentional about it. Don't let relationships wane and drop away without knowing why. Don't fail to appreciate a changing relationship for what it is. And don't forget to be grateful for every one of those amazing friends, lovers, and others who have made you the person you are—the person who can conceive, design, develop, and successfully grow an amazing business.

Significance, Success, and Legacy: New Meanings, New Opportunities, and New Adventures

ViBI again!

Remember early in the book when we discussed the critical role that you play in the intentional design of the future, and how stating an intention helped you focus your Vision-inspired Big Idea into a successful business?

That same attention to Integrity, Intuition, and creative focus can help you discover new ways to engage and allow your vision to "live" again. What you learn along the way can expand your vision in new directions and keep the ViBI process alive and energized.

Even while you are in the middle of growing and scaling your business, we believe that you should begin living and planning for your ViBI's next future. Over and over we have heard—and believe with our entire beings—that success comes from believing in success, and the most impactful way to believe in your own success is to visualize it. So get specific about your second life (or third or thirtieth, if you are a serial entrepreneur), and factor that into your thinking and dreaming process.

You've already accomplished incredible things with your business and have begun to define the ways that the *unique character* that is *you* can make a difference in the world. Whether that is by changing lives, creating fabulous workplaces, sharing profit, creating new and innovative products, or sharing what you've learned, if you take the initiative and time to begin shaping that next big thing now, you will find that you are inspired and fresh, and even the hardest days of growing a business will be made easier.

Paying It Forward—Starting Now

We have been amazed at how willing women are to help each other as entrepreneurs. Sure, we've occasionally come across women who have succumbed to the idea that "I'm too busy, too smart, too paranoid, or too special" to help others, but it's rare.

What we more often see are women who consistently underestimate how much they have to share and the power that their learning and insight will have for other SmartGirls. And we meet many women who would like to help but don't know how or where to begin.

> *How can you use your entrepreneurial strengths and your SmartGirls Ways to expand or multiply the impact you can have and pay it forward to help others?*

There are many ways for you to share what you have learned, expand on the knowledge you've gained, and make a difference. There is also a particular mind-set that helps you be successful. We're going to touch on a few that we believe can make a difference in terms of paying it forward to other women entrepreneurs.

› Step up as a role model.
› Share your story.
› Mentor as much as you can.
› Invest.

Embracing Your Role as a Role Model

Through our hundreds of discussions with successful women—from teachers to talent agents, billon-dollar business owners to basketball players—we hear over and over the clear desire to give back. Many of these women have chosen charities and worthwhile causes to throw their considerable knowledge behind, fitting that work into their busy business and family lives.

For us, there is no greater way for a woman entrepreneur to give back than by understanding this one simple truth: *Sharing your story,* your success, breakdowns, and breakthroughs serves as a significant inspiration to other women entrepreneurs and to the girls and women who want a life that offers them more opportunity for success, financial independence, self-respect, and control over their lives.

The more that women share their stories, the more opportunity there is for others to see themselves succeeding as entrepreneurs—there will be someone, probably several someones, who relate not only to your particular story, but also to the personal challenges and barriers that you had to overcome to succeed.

Most entrepreneurs are tapped into networks or forums for sharing locally. If you are not, we encourage you to do so. This direct storytelling is critical. But since women entrepreneurs are also very busy, the commitment to share and mentor can become daunting. That's why we have created the 100x100 Project as an inspiration vehicle. This storytelling element of our website is specifically focused on building a web of stories so that anyone who goes looking there will find someone to inspire her.

> On our website, we have a special location for success stories. Inspiration matters. Direct experience makes it real. Tell us your story or submit the story of amazing women entrepreneurs you know. We'd love to help you spread the word.
>
> (www.SmartGirlsWay.com/stories)

Mentor

Even more important than sharing stories is the specific, practical, and consistent (even if periodic) act of mentoring through advice and insights.

When looking at the ecosystem for women entrepreneurs, it's clear that there are many gaps. Many great organizations are currently evaluating how to close these gaps and make a difference.

For us, there are two things that don't require study as much as action. It's clear that women need other women to step up, *mentor,* and *invest.* Women tell us that what's missing for them are easy and effective mentoring aids, in particular the kinds that will let you build a relationship and take the exchange beyond empathy to true mentorship. Mentoring is more than just gathering information and insights. Mentoring is about knowing enough about another woman's ViBI or business and the current challenges she is facing to make a difference with directed input. It's not about advising, but about sharing insights, engaging in appreciative inquiry, and directing attention to specific ways of solving, or at least looking at, problems.

In the meantime, the quick tips are to keep it simple, keep it small, and keep it focused. Keep the approach and opportunity simple. Set a coffee date with women who want your insight; dedicate a blog entry once or twice a month to topics you are often asked about; create a way for women to engage with you in small groups. When you're mentoring, stay on topic (yes, we are great at Weaving, but if you have a precious hour or two to mentor, you want to walk away thinking you made a difference).

Invest

Perhaps the biggest gap to close is financial confidence. At the outset, women in start-up mode need to understand their finance options and then confidently obtain the money. Confidence also plays a role in the investment of women in other women. By and large, women entrepreneurs watch their male counterparts to see where to invest—and therefore end up investing in male-led companies of equal or lesser upside potential than the women-owned and women-led companies coming across their thresholds. This is often true even in the "angel investor" groups formed specifically to focus on women.

The only antidote is for women to step up and address this quiet prejudice through action. This is a case where the control is in your hands more than ever before. Investing in women entrepreneurs *is* investing in the future. We have a problem. We are out of relationship to each other, the planet, and future generations. But we have an answer, and that answer is to give the feminine voice of society a parity position in the creation of our future. For that to happen, the barriers—real and perceived—must be lifted, and we can do it.

We can lift each other as we climb—now!

Let the same Passion that allowed you to overcome all odds and move to success with your own business drive you to invest and engage in the success of other women. You are a smart, savvy, and sensational SmartGirl. You don't need a nod from a man to invest and bring another company to success. Just do it!

Be Defined by Momentum

Going back to our bridge metaphor, the first steps matter, but keeping momentum matters most. Momentum and forward motion are your friends. Women sometimes tell us they don't know what the next step should be—whether they are starting a business, scaling it, or looking for a post-entrepreneurial next step. Usually, though, after spending some time talking about it, even if they may not know exactly what that next step is, they do know in which direction it should be headed.

And it should be *always* be forward.

Don't retrench or second-guess. Make a new move. *Forward.* Take a research project. *Forward.* Take a bigger leap. *Forward.* Moving avoids the risk of standing in the middle of a bridge that might start swaying at any time. Even if you change your ViBI or business model completely, you have to *move* to get across the bridge.

Gore Vidal said, "In writing and politicking it's best not to think about it—just do it." We believe that is even more true for entrepreneurs.

Nike is the goddess of victory. It is also the name of the company that started off with a couple of track-and-field coaches literally making shoes using waffle irons to improve the performance of their athletes. But their slogan isn't about victory. It's *Just do it.* What Nike understood might be what we have come to understand in studying entrepreneurship, and especially women entrepreneurs.

It is in the *doing* that the momentum is found.

It is in the *doing* that the inspiration is discovered.

It is in the *doing* that greatness is born.

And it is in the doing *that the **victory is defined**.*

Real SmartGirls Way Stories

In conjunction with writing this book, we came to believe that shifting the cultural barriers to entrepreneurial success for women required shifting the dialogue from a focus on *fixing problems* to a focus on *finding working solutions*. To do this, we spoke with women entrepreneurs at all stages in a broad range of industries—from technology and new energy to consumer goods and new media sectors—about the key skills and support systems that enabled their success. The specific input and insights gleaned directly from all of these women entrepreneurs pointed to a particular set of characteristics and critical success factors outlined in this book.

It also led to the creation of the 100×100 Project—the first SmartGirls Way initiative celebrating the strengths and successes of women entrepreneurs. Jean and Tracey and other members of their team grabbed their cameras and traveled across the country to speak with women at all stages of entrepreneurship. We were surprised and inspired by how willing these women were not only to tell us their great stories, but also to open up their networks and nominate other great women whose ViBIs and businesses they admired.

These interviews helped us to clarify how women build businesses based on their strengths of character, hard work, and conviction. We so admire the many ambitious and beneficial products, services, and technologies that women are bringing to the world.

We chose twelve of the women from the 100×100 Project to illustrate the SmartGirls Way Methodology in this book. Their complete stories are below. In addition to Elizabeth Bennett, Michelle King Robson, Ce Ce Chin, Janice Shade, Sarah McIlroy, Amra Tareen, Gretchen Schauffler, Heidi Ganahl, Stephanie Allen, Jane Hoffer, Sheryl O'Loughlin, and Sharon Lechter, there are many more women making amazing contributions to our world who are featured in the 2011 100×100 Project. View their stories and pass them on at www.SmartGirlsWay.com.

We believe that nothing proves a point better than showing examples of it. So by sharing these stories, we hope not only that you'll gain insights and an understanding of the lessons learned by others (so that maybe you don't have to), but most important, that you'll gain the confidence to share your entrepreneurial vision and story.

We are extremely grateful for the women of the 100×100 Project. They have given us more than just their time; they have helped us weave together a network that is more than just great stories. It's the heartbeat of a movement!

Elizabeth's Story

Elizabeth Bennett
Founder, Africa Direct
Denver, Colorado

Year Founded: 1994	Number of Employees: 7	Entrepreneurial Stage: 3

SmartGirls Strengths: Passion & Integrity

Elizabeth Bennett is a serial entrepreneur. After spending eight years in international franchising for the McDonald's Corporation, she then embarked on her own franchising venture. Unfortunately, the venture failed, and Elizabeth found herself taking a career break. At the same time, she and her life partner, Sara Luther, a professional squash player, were raising five children, four of whom were adopted African-Americans. The couple was active in anti-apartheid politics, and when Nelson Mandela was elected president of South Africa in 1994, they decided it was time for a massive revitalization of energy. They took their three youngest children out of school and moved to southern Africa for eight months. While touring the countries of Lesotho, Mozambique, Zimbabwe, Botswana, and Swaziland in a renovated camper van, Elizabeth and Sara realized they were buying more African jewelry and art than they could ever give away or appreciate themselves. Upon returning home, they started to host shows and open houses to sell the wares, and soon had a $50,000-a-year business.

Yet Elizabeth realized that if she was going to really provide an income for her growing family—and more directly contribute to the local economy of the Africans who had created the artifacts—she would need to quickly expand her market, staff, and distribution model.

Her Vision-inspired Big Idea

For Elizabeth, this sparked the beginning of a new era for Africa Direct. "I am a serial entrepreneur, and I've built my success on learning from both success and failure," she explains. "You only get to have a fresh set of eyes about your business once, and then you need to give yourself an MBA equivalent (if you don't already have one) in technology and finance. For me, that meant paying attention to this growing e-commerce trend called eBay. When your market hits you over the head, you're wise if you notice it. It was luck that eBay was just taking off at the time, and it was the missing piece for my Vision."

Moving to a virtual business model allowed the company to cultivate buyers throughout the world, including gallery owners, art collectors, academics, and museums as well as everyday consumers. Elizabeth kept the pricing of her goods accessible, from under $50 to several thousand dollars for some one-of-a-kind pieces.

Elizabeth and Sara also invested time in creating operating principles that were in alignment with their personal values such as "Do well by doing good" and "Be honest and legal." These principles have guided the business over its sixteen years and helped it to build relationships only with those buyers whom Elizabeth and Sara trusted and felt were acting in the best interest of the artisans.

In 2009, at *Fortune*'s 50 Most Powerful Women in Business Summit, Elizabeth was one of five entrepreneurs honored as top women business owners. "My biggest single takeaway from the *Fortune* Top 50 event was that the one thing we could do to help the local and national economy was to create a job."

The couple hired a Congolese-born and internationally trained PhD in African art to be their curator. "We made some changes in our corporate cultures to bring Niangi on," Elizabeth says, "but we felt she was critical to the integrity of our business. When you realize the implications your business decisions can have on the world we live in, hard business decisions become good business decisions."

Today, Elizabeth and Sara are top eBay sellers who support hundreds of African artists and craftspeople. They still operate their $1.2 million business out of their home, where the garage is the office and the basement holds a vast inventory of art, artifacts, jewelry, baskets, masks, carvings, and textiles.

The company continues to live by its mission to *do well by doing good*. To that end, Africa Direct buyers and sellers have raised more than $70,000 for like causes via eBay Giving Works, and Elizabeth donates consulting time to various nonprofits. Learn more about Elizabeth and her company at www.AfricaDirect.com.

Michelle's Story

Michelle King Robson
Founder, EmpowHER
Scottsdale, Arizona

Year Founded: 2007	Number of Employees: 22	Entrepreneurial Stage: 3

SmartGirls Strengths: Passion, Intuition, & Weaving

Michelle King Robson credits her success at the top of one of the most empowering health and wellness sites for women to her passion, her intuition, and her ability to share and weave great support systems.

In 2003, Michelle faced down a debilitating health issue that left her feeling helpless and alone. She did not know at the time that she was suffering from what had been an undiagnosed case of severe hormonal imbalance and perimenopause, and thus spent several frustrating and painful years while doctors treated symptoms without finding a real solution to her condition. After reaching rock bottom, when she could no longer get out of bed and even contemplated suicide, Michelle's doctor encouraged her to advocate for herself, and she started reading and researching on her own—eventually coming upon a new hormone therapy that got her back on her feet.

"At first I felt tremendous relief, and then...I got angry," explains Michelle. "I decided that never again would I allow another woman to go through what I had gone through."

Her Vision-inspired Big Idea

Michelle decided that the most empowering thing she could do for herself and others was to create an online forum where women could get the information they needed to make informed decisions and take control over their own health management.

An experienced philanthropist, Michelle gathered advisors she knew and quickly put together a website backed by an advisory board of some of the most well-known physicians and experts in the field of medicine. She also made an integrity decision that would shape the future of her site:

"We decided early on that we were going to be open, not closed. Some websites draw you in and keep you; we wanted to be open and get people to where they needed to be."

Today, EmpowHER provides women with the most comprehensive and up-to-date information available on women's health and is a world-class forum for women to connect and share stories of struggle and hope. Michelle remains a leader in health advocacy and recently led the second largest write-in campaign in FDA history for drugs and treatments for women's health. EmpowHER has won numerous awards and receives over 1.5 million visitors per month, with another 7 to 8 million viewers through syndication of EmpowHER's women's health and wellness content across the Web.

Learn more about Michelle at www.EmpowerHER.com.

Ce Ce's Story

Ce Ce Chin
Founder, 80%20 Shoes
New York, New York

Year Founded: 2005	Number of Employees: 4	Entrepreneurial Stage: 3

SmartGirls Strengths: Curiosity & Passion

Ce Ce Chin can trace her dream to move to New York City and be a fashion designer all the way back to her ninth birthday: "I asked for Fashion Plates for my birthday. This was an artsy toy; by using several interchangeable tracing plates, you could create an image of a woman in various fashionable outfits."

From that moment on, her creativity and curiosity were fulfilled by her passion for design. She often played "wardrobe therapy" by composing outfits from borrowed items from her parents' and older sisters' closets. Later, as an adult developing her career in New York, she worked as a handbag designer with some of the most celebrated brand names in fashion: DKNY, Michael Kors, and Calvin Klein.

While refining her design aesthetic from these leaders, Ce Ce developed an understanding of the market and an eye for what's to come. Confident that she had the vision to develop a line of her own, Ce Ce played the game of risk and stepped out to create her first collection.

Her Vision-inspired Big Idea

While experimenting with her own designs, Ce Ce caught her first big break when her initial idea for a hand-painted slip-on sneaker was previewed in the online fashion site DailyCandy. The coverage from the fashion website resulted in such a large flood of emails inquiring about her shoes that she was inspired to leave her full-time job to pursue her shoe company. Her first move was an entire collection of graphic slip-ons that was picked up by Urban Outfitters for nationwide distribution.

Curiosity continued to drive the creation of her business. "For me, designing is not so much about sitting down at a desk, but about being out in the world and noticing how people express themselves through their own style," Ce Ce says. "I might sketch shoes on napkins or receipts while doing this; then, there's the basis for my design. One of the things I found inspiring was the physical relationship shoes have with travel; that's something I've always found exciting. I love the way shoes can take a woman across a neighborhood or across the world; there is something very romantic about that."

With her keen eye for fashion, Ce Ce observed that women really wear 20 percent of their wardrobe items—their favorites—80 percent of the time. This became the driving principle of her brand: developing comfortable and fashionable core favorites. As a brand, 80%20 developed a loyal following almost immediately.

The vision for the ultimate shoe came from personal experience. "Petite women like me often want more of a heel in our everyday footwear," Ce Ce says. In her sophomore collection, she introduced a hidden-wedge shoe—the wedge placed inside a flat-boot silhouette. It made 80%20 famous in new markets, taking the brand beyond the sneaker concept as the style resonated in markets where sneakers were normally absent.

Since then, Ce Ce's work has been covered by some of the most important fashion magazines and worn by celebrities around the world. When she's not designing shoes and running her empire, her travels and personal life provide ample opportunity to fuel her curiosity. From surfing to vintage pop culture and fashion iconography, Ce Ce is always aware of the smallest nuance or moment that could become her next inspiration.

Janice's Story

Janice Shade
Founder, TrueBody Products
Richmond, Vermont

Year Founded: 2008	Number of Employees: 3	Entrepreneurial Stage: 2

SmartGirls Strengths: Intuition & Integrity

After securing an MBA in corporate strategy from the Yale School of Management, and a BS in finance from Boston University, Janice Shade had a successful career in product management with consumer manufacturing leaders Procter & Gamble and Welch's. While she loved working with big brands, there came a time when she wanted to work on products that were more closely aligned with her personal values and lifelong commitment to the environment. So she found her way to leadership roles at Nelson Bach—maker of Rescue Remedy, Bach Flower Essences, and Nelsons Homeopathy—and eventually to Seventh Generation, the national leader in natural household products. While at Seventh Generation, she held the role of marketing director but playfully took the title of "Nature Girl," honing her product-management expertise for the natural consumer market and playing an influential role in that company's evolution as a socially responsible business leader.

Her Vision-inspired Big Idea

After the birth of her second daughter, Janice was looking for her next opportunity and experimented with consulting. During this time, she became increasingly troubled by the high price of natural/organic products. When a friend came to her with an idea for a bar soap he called "natural Dial," her commitment to the environment and her expertise in product management collided in an intuitive hit.

"I knew in my gut it was a good idea," explains Janice. "I had been a part of so many new products in my career, and I just felt this was a terrific concept because you shouldn't have to be wealthy to be healthy."

Janice and two partners started developing a business plan and creating soap samples, but after a while, both partners decided they needed to pursue other paid jobs. However, Janice remained committed to the idea of all-natural soap at an affordable price because it was something she wanted for her own family and believed in for the world. So she bought her two partners out of their shares and made plans to liquidate her 401(k) to bootstrap her business.

Getting funding was the primary challenge to launching TrueBody Products, and she began to seek advice from her network, including her former boss at Seventh Generation.

"I met with Jeffrey to seek his advice on finding investors. I expected him to give me some guidance, but he completely surprised me by offering to become my first investor," she says.

Janice took over full-time management of TrueBody Products in the winter of 2008 and launched her first soap nine months later. She was able to tap her relationships from her product-management days to put the product onto the shelves while simultaneously courting the angel investment community, building a team, and aligning an advisory board comprised of some of her most trusted advisors.

Today, TrueBody Products are sold in over three hundred stores across the country, and Janice is working on expanding her product line from bath and facial soaps to include liquid soap, body wash, and shampoo.

Learn more about Janice at www.TrueBodyProducts.com.

Sarah's Story

Sarah McIlroy		
FashionPlaytes		
Beverly, Massachusetts		
Year Founded: 2008	Number of Employees: 15	Entrepreneurial Stage: 2
SmartGirls Strengths: Intuition & Creativity		

As a child, Sarah McIlroy always had a knack for creativity, intuitively applied to her own sense of style. Some of her fondest childhood memories are of the days she spent with her mother creating her own clothing designs, which her mother would then sew for her.

Sarah's first job out of college was as a product-development manager for the Foreside Company, where she developed high-end decorative accessories and home-furnishing products that appear in retail stores and catalogs, including Crate & Barrel, Neiman Marcus, Bloomingdale's, and Horchow. Over the next fifteen years, Sarah evolved her experience in design and marketing, working for major brands such as Brookstone, Atari, Hasbro Interactive, and eventually Midway Amusement Games. At the same time, she was also nurturing three young children, and she began to reminisce about the bonding time she and her mother had experienced through sewing all those years ago.

Sarah's background in the arts and creating great design and interactive gaming activities for children collided in 2008 when she started toying with the idea of an e-commerce site where girls aged five through twelve could create—and wear—their own clothing designs.

Her Vision-inspired Big Idea

Sarah ran the idea for what would become FashionPlaytes by her sister, a mother of four girls.

"She said, 'My girls spend hours online, and they would flip out if they could do this themselves,'" Sarah remembers. "That conversation was the catalyst that helped me leave my high-paying job and strike out on my own."

Her business experience contributed to her desire to be a first-mover in this space. As a child, Sarah, like Ce Ce Chin and many other girls, had owned a Fashion Plates design kit. The popular toy of the 1980s allowed a girl to pick different pieces of an outfit (tops and bottoms) to create different designs and then do pencil rubbings over the plates to create customized looks. Building on the iconic concept, Sarah started researching how girls could choose from various basics (such as tops, bottoms, jackets, and accessories) and customize them to their own tastes and style. The most important element of the process was that the girls could actually wear what they had designed, so she started researching factories to determine how she could deliver an affordable finished product at a reasonable price.

Her first move was to find a cofounder. Mary Beth Tirrell had important manufacturing connections (as well as a daughter in their target demographic), and together they began to pitch their idea to angel investors and venture capitalists. In 2009, Sarah secured $1.5 million in seed funding, and by the end of that year, FashionPlaytes.com launched to the public. It wasn't long before the company was receiving accolades from not only girls and their parents but the press, winning several prestigious awards.

While growing her business, Sarah struggled to find ways to balance her lifestyle. Staying true to her vision of creating a bonding experience for mothers and girls, she found ways to bring her own daughters into the business.

"I felt it was really important to involve my girls in the business so they could see not just how their own clothing creations could come to life, but also how you can follow a dream and build something from the ground up," Sarah says. "So I started asking them what they liked in clothing and including them in the design of our product offering. We realized pretty quickly how valuable it was having the insights from my daughters, so much so that their involvement helped us to create a girl-influenced advisory group that helps us derive our new product mix."

In October 2010, FashionPlaytes raised an additional $4 million in a private equity funding round. The company also received a 2010 Mom's Choice Award for outstanding product, and in 2011, InternetRetailer.com named FashionPlaytes on its annual Hot 100 E-Retailer list.

The next step for Sarah was to incorporate an online gaming platform into the FashionPlaytes experience.

Today, the company continues to gain attention from publications such as the *Huffington Post, Redbook, Family Circle, Good Housekeeping,* the *Boston Globe,* and others for its unique social-commerce business model and gaming platform. The company has also been featured on shows such as the *CBS Early Show,* which featured the company's young designers by showcasing their creations on television segments nationwide.

You can learn more about Sarah at www.FashionPlaytes.com.

Amra's Story

Amra Tareen
Founder & CEO, AllVoices.com
San Francisco, California

Year Founded: 2007	In 2011, AllVoices.com was purchased by Datran Media, a New York City–based digital marketing technology company.	Entrepreneurial Stage: 3

SmartGirls Strengths: Passion & Integrity

Amra Tareen is a global aggregator of knowledge and people. Born in Pakistan and raised in Australia, Amra came to the United States to attend Harvard Business School. She earned her leadership stripes in the telecommunications and technology industry before joining Sevin Rosen Funds as a partner focused on investment opportunities in the communications infrastructure and next-generation carriers.

She might have stayed on the venture-capital path indefinitely had it not been for 9/11 and the ensuing climate that left her, a Muslim mother of two young boys in San Francisco, disheartened by what she perceived as a growing media bias toward Muslims.

Her Vision-inspired Big Idea

Amra's frustration with the media's portrayal of Muslims took root during a volunteer relief mission she made to Pakistan after the devastating

2005 earthquake. "I was on the ground for a short period of time, but the resilience of the people inspired me. I wanted to share my experience so the rest of the world could see what was really happening on the ground, but there was no way to effectively communicate this," she said. "I had pictures of the destruction and amazing stories of heroism and compassion, but I didn't know how I was going to get this message out. I didn't think I would get a response from CNN, and I didn't want to write a blog that nobody would ever find."

She realized that a social-media platform that allowed people to report on-the-ground activities for the rest of the world would fill an unmet need for an unbiased, real-time view of important local activities.

"This inspired me to start a company that would let anyone, no matter where they are, report on what they knew about an event, upload photos, videos, and express their views for a global audience. We quickly realized that in addition to sharing, every voice needs context so that readers can understand the viewpoint and add content to it—similar to Wikipedia."

Amra's passion to create a platform that represented all voices became the driving force as she started and then grew her company from an idea to the world's largest global community offering of citizen-led journalism in three years.

Hiring people who believed as strongly in her vision as she did was one of the reasons that she was able to secure over $9 million in venture capital during the heart of the 2009 financial crisis. "The team is the most important part of building a successful company. Without a team who shared my vision, my idea would have just remained...a good idea," Amra says.

In the spring of 2011, AllVoices was acquired by Datran Media, a New York City–based digital marketing technology company. Today, AllVoices has more than 440,000 citizen reporters from over 180 countries. Amra remains as senior vice president of Datran Media at the parent-company level.

"AllVoices was an evolutionary process for me," she says, "where I grew from a focus of 'me' to a focus on a global 'we,' and I continue to be driven by the global impact of our mission."

Learn more about Amra at www.AllVoices.com.

Gretchen's Story

Gretchen Schauffler
Founder, Devine Color
Lake Oswego, Oregon

| Year Founded: 1996 | In 2010, Gretchen sold her company to Valspar. She remains the creativity spearhead of the brand. | Entrepreneurial Stage: 3 |

SmartGirls Strengths: Curiosity & Creativity

Gretchen Schauffler has always had a creative flair and a curious mind. She attributes much of this to a childhood that challenged her to be curious in her constant travels between her family's homes in Puerto Rico and rural Oregon, and to her exposure to the color and diversity that comes from living in two vastly different cultures.

In fact, creativity and curiosity are the two ingredients that, when mixed with color, took Gretchen from being a suburban housewife with a knack for interior design to the creator and owner of one of the Northwest's most unique and environmentally friendly paint lines.

Her Vision-inspired Big Idea

While living in suburban Oregon and raising her children, Gretchen—like many women in the early '90s—had left a corporate life to live the role of domestic CEO at the height of the 1990s Martha Stewart era. Paint color became a way to express her creativity, and she started mixing unique and vibrant colors on her walls that reflected her dualistic Caribbean and Pacific Northwest heritage.

"People would come to me and ask, 'How did you come up with that color?' or say 'I want that,' and so I started mixing custom colors for other people," explains Gretchen. "I knew then that I wanted to help people create beautiful, colorful environments that bring balance and beauty to their lives, so I started to create my own line of custom paint colors."

Gretchen's business as a color consultant took off, and she started getting larger jobs and referrals. Then, a 6,000-square-foot mistake forced her to make a dramatic change in her business: "I had the paint company mix my custom color, and it came out awful. It looked sweaty on the walls, it was oily and hard to put on, and I realized, *if you can't guarantee the quality and consistency of the paint, you can't control or guarantee your custom color.*"

This was the beginning of a curious journey that led her to search for a paint that would live up to her vision—paint with a rich and creamy texture that was easy to use and felt like yogurt. After a year of searching, she realized, if you can't find what you're looking for, make it!

Her quest led her to approach Oregon's legendary Miller Paint Company, which was hoping to reach a new target audience: women. Gretchen sold them on her idea for a new textured paint line and went on to develop innovative marketing approaches to color, including a two-ounce paint sample, the Mini-Paint Pouch, that revolutionized the paint industry and changed the way large companies market and sample color to women.

Today, Gretchen is one of the Northwest's top women in the male-dominated paint industry, and Miller Paint continues to be the exclusive regional manufacturer and distributor of the original Devine Delicate Wall Finish, along with Devine Powder Wall Finish, and Devine Luscious Wall Finish. There's also a new line of exterior paint that has the look and feel of leather, whose brand promises, "The Wisdom of a Woman Inside Every Can." But she's not stopping there. In 2010, Valspar, a national and global leader in paint manufacturing, acquired Devine Color as a stand-alone boutique brand. Gretchen continues to creatively spearhead the brand. This fall, Devine Color will be the first ever paint to be sold on the Home Shopping Network and at HSN.com. She has also published *Karma Physics: What Happens to You When "They Should'a Known Better"*, a book based on a philosophy and process aimed at helping people free themselves of misery when they encounter conflict in intrapersonal relationships by acknowledging and meeting their essential need for trust and confidence in their relationships.

Learn more about Gretchen at www.DevineColor.com.

Heidi's Story

Heidi Ganahl Founder, Camp Bow Wow Boulder, Colorado		
Year Founded: 2000	**Number of Employees:** 200 franchise locations; 30 corporate employees and 2,500 staff in 200 franchise locations	Entrepreneurial Stage: 3
SmartGirls Strengths: Passion & Integrity		

Heidi Ganahl has always had a passion for animals. In 1994, she and her husband, frustrated by the lack of a suitable pet-care facility for their two dogs, decided, *if you can't find it, build it*. At the time, the concept of doggy day care had just started taking off around the country. Together, they created a business plan for Camp Bow Wow and started looking for facilities. Then, Heidi's husband was killed in a small-plane crash, and her life changed dramatically, teaching Heidi a great deal about channeling passion to overcome obstacles. Five years later, she returned to the business plan and turned her lifelong love of dogs into her life's work.

Her Vision-inspired Big Idea

Heidi took the remaining settlement money from her husband's accident and invested it into the Camp Bow Wow dream. Heidi's vision for her first facility, which opened in Denver in 2000, was that it be a place where a dog could be a dog. This premise involved access to both indoor and outdoor play, constant socialization, and webcam access for pet owners so they could check up on their furry friends at their leisure.

"Integrity was a driving force in my vision from the very beginning," she says. "What we are is all about the animals, and making sure they have a healthy, happy, safe experience. My motto has always been, *Don't put the dollar before the dog*."

Within a year, she had opened a second location, and a year after that, she started franchising the business. Growing and scaling Camp Bow Wow from a small business to an enterprise required an entirely different set of skills and needs.

"At one point during our growth, every member of my family was either on my board or working within the business, and I learned then the value of weaving together a strong support system," explains Heidi. "This support system also included some great mentors in the franchise industry who donated their time to the business, as well as my own clients at the camps whose feedback and expertise on their pets shaped my business."

Passion for her vision and the animals she cared for carried her through a rapid growth phase. That passion became a source of credibility and confidence when seeking capital or bringing on new franchisees to her brand: "I wasn't going to compromise with the quality of care in our franchise business; we have an extensive criteria for all of our operators. If we take care of our animals then the parents of our furry friends will also be happy with the brand and that will benefit our franchisees."

A little over a decade later, Camp Bow Wow is a $50 million business with 111 franchise locations (over 200 sold) in forty states and Canada. Heidi continues to rely on her integrity and passion to grow and enhance her business and has also started the Bow Wow Buddies Foundation, which aids animal shelters and research to end cancer in canines. To date, Bow Wow Buddies has raised over $1 million for local pet charities nationwide, assisted in the adoption of more than five thousand dogs, and contributed over $50,000 in grants via its "On Our Way Home" extreme makeover project for shelters.

"We want to take all we've learned about building these premier facilities and support animal shelters as they build better facilities and integrate play that makes animals more adoptable," she says.

Learn more about Heidi at www.Heidi-Inc.com.

Stephanie's Story

Stephanie Allen
Dream Dinners
Snohomish, Washington

Year Founded:	Number of Employees:	Entrepreneurial Stage:
2002	105 national franchises	3

SmartGirls Strengths: Weaving & Intuition

Named the "grandmother" of fix-and-freeze businesses by *Time* magazine, Stephanie Allen attributes the creation of Dream Dinners to the SmartGirls Way characteristic of weaving. Allen says, "Dream Dinners was created by weaving. Women like to get together to get something done." As a mother, a business owner, and a long-time member of the international service organization Mothers of Preschoolers, Stephanie had firsthand insight into the trials and tensional pulls that women experience when trying to balance a full lifestyle with a healthy, family-oriented meal.

"I feel it is important for families and friends to get together around the dinner table for a home-cooked meal for one hour, two to five nights a week to foster and develop relationships, and I was inspired to find a solution to the ongoing dinnertime dilemma," she says.

Her Vision-inspired Big Idea

Like most working moms, Stephanie struggled to balance the demands of her catering business with the needs of her family. She used her culinary background and created fix-and-freeze meals one night a week that lasted for an entire month for her family. This process worked wonderfully for Stephanie for seven years. And the word began to spread around her small town. She decided to open her catering kitchen one night a month to friends and family so they could have a girls' night out and provide their families with a month's worth of home-cooked meals. Little did she know that another busy professional mom and friend, Tina Kuna, would also find the value in her concept and ultimately become her co-founder. "We didn't think of it as a business at all; we just wanted to help our friends and family get dinner on the table," she says.

Stephanie improved on traditional precooked methods, resulting in better-tasting meals. She refined the process and efficiency, and began developing a collection of specialized recipes. She continued to be showered with requests to share her method for time-saving meal preparation. In 2002, when the demand became overwhelming, Stephanie sought support from Tina, and the two friends pooled personal savings and applied for a business loan from the Small Business Administration to open the first Dream Dinners store. Within a year, the company had expanded regionally, and the partners began receiving thousands of unsolicited franchise inquires. In 2003, they expanded their business model and established a national franchise program. In less than three years, Dream Dinners expanded from an idea to help their families and friends make their lives easier to a thriving national brand.

Weaving continued to play a critical role as Stephanie and Tina selected franchise operators, seeking out other business owners with a similar mission to promote healthy family eating and a desire to make a positive impact on the world. "Even more important than our business model or the training of our franchise operators was the commitment to helping moms get dinner on the table." Stephanie says. "We built that philosophy into everything we did, from our franchise application to our core values, and used it to build a Dream Dinners community."

To date, Dream Dinners serves more than 700,000 fix-and-freeze servings nationally per month. For Stephanie, the next milestone for her company is to hit 1 million meals per month, but her personal focus is getting families together at the dinner table over a home-cooked meal. She points out, "Eating a home-cooked meal two to five times a week is a start. Creating a supportive family infrastructure—that is our real focus." To that end, Stephanie and Tina have just finished a book, *The Hour That Matters*, to help families create and foster relationships around the dinner table.

For more on Dream Dinners, visit www.DreamDinners.com.

Jane's Story

Jane Hoffer
Cofounder, Ohanarama.com
Philadelphia, Pennsylvania

Year Founded: 2009	Number of Employees: Fewer than 10	Entrepreneurial Stage: 2

SmartGirls Strengths: Intuition & Integrity

After the sale of her first company, Prescient Systems, in 2009, Jane Hoffer took some time off to enjoy her young family and ponder her next big move. She realized that some of her fondest memories of her childhood were of the hours spent around the table playing games with her grandparents, who lived just ten miles away. Many years later when Jane's own parents came to visit her children from Florida, the games came out again, and new family memories were created. The concept of "family togetherness" through games was the concept behind Ohanarama, a social gaming platform designed to bring extended families living across geographies closer together. *Ohanarama* is a Hawaiian word for "family," and it was inspired by one of her children's favorite movies, *Lilo & Stitch*, where family means no one is left behind or forgotten.

Her Vision-inspired Big Idea

As a parent, Jane noticed that there was a gap between the social gaming platforms for children and families, specifically for that six-to-nine-years age group who were somewhat independent but still required a great deal of supervision and support online. The year was 2009, and Facebook was becoming a social-networking phenomena.

Jane felt that her children, like all of the grandchildren of the nearly 50 percent of grandparents who live more than 200 miles away, were missing out on some of that social family time she had grown up with, and she intuitively felt that there was an opportunity to change this dynamic. So Jane started looking at technology, children's gaming, and social networking. She realized there was a gap nobody was addressing. "The original social networks were the extended family living close together. Nobody was connecting the distance-based extended family through game play and using that natural social network of families to improve the relationships across distance in a meaningful way," she explains.

Her first step was to find a business partner with gaming and educational technology expertise who could augment her business strengths. Through her research, she finally found the ideal candidate in Barton Listick. "I actually made a cold call to him in the beginning and explained my vision. We started talking, and eventually he joined me as a partner in my business," she says.

Together, Jane and Barton realized that they didn't have the capital or time to build their own gaming site from scratch, so they made two strategic decisions that shaped the future of Ohanarama. The first was the decision to license existing low-point-of-entry content on their site so that they could focus their talent and resources on developing family trivia and interactive activities that provided more meaningful engagements. The second decision was to leverage Facebook's existing social network with a gaming plug-in rather than try to build their own stand-alone website.

After raising initial angel investment, Jane took the Ohanarama story on the road, pitching it to venture capitalists and industry veterans, who often tried to pigeonhole them into other Facebook games. "It took nearly twelve months before I finally, albeit skeptically, took yet another networking call through which I received an introduction to Charles Huang, the cofounder of Guitar Hero. He became one of our initial gaming industry investors and now sits on our board of advisors," Jane says.

Today, Ohanarama is the go-to place for multigenerational families online. Jane is also focused on expanding the Ohanarama platform to other disconnected multinational, multicultural families to create a fun social gaming platform that brings families together.

Learn more about Jane at www.ohanarama.com.

Sheryl's Story

Sheryl O'Loughlin Founder, Nest Collective Emeryville, California		
Year Founded: 2007	**Number of Employees:** 30+	**Entrepreneurial Stage:** 3
SmartGirls Strengths: Integrity & Passion		

Sheryl O'Loughlin is a social entrepreneur with a passion for healthy eating. She nurtured this passion throughout her career at Clif Bar & Company, holding several leadership positions including head of marketing (where she spearheaded the creation of the LUNA Bar), and three years as the company's chief executive officer. After ten years of contributing to the company's rise as one of the leading manufacturers of organic energy and nutritional foods for people on the move, Sheryl decided she wanted to devote her time to the next phase of her life.

"I've been passionate about healthy food my whole life, and that passion guided my professional evolution," she says. "At Clif, I was an athlete with a passion for healthy eating, and LUNA Bar was the natural iteration of that. When I had kids, my passion for healthy eating remained, but my goals shifted towards caring for my children and a personal desire to do something about childhood obesity. We are raising the first generation of children who could die at a younger age than their parents. Healthy eating is a critical aspect in this issue, and I had a burning desire to do something about it."

Her Vision-inspired Big Idea

In 2007 while attending the Natural Products Exposition, Sheryl and her co-founder, Neil Grimmer, realized that no one was addressing the market of healthy food for kids in a way that fit the modern family's busy lifestyle. She'd had a similar epiphany she had in her days as CEO of Clif Bar: "The idea for the LUNA Bar came from seeking a solution. Women weren't using the energy bar category at the time because no company was addressing their needs. With kids it was the same thing. Modern parents need a nutritious and portable option for their children. Kids want things to taste good and if it looks cool it will appeal to them. It seemed an obvious solution to redesign kids' experience with healthy food products so that they would embrace healthy food."

With this focus, Sheryl and Neil founded Nest Collective, a company that would make healthy food for busy families with products for early childhood—from high chair to lunch box. The partners decided the fastest way to spread their social mission was to acquire existing companies that already had a devoted consumer base and high food integrity. This would allow them to leverage their collective talent in innovation and design to create a better consumer experience for the modern family lifestyle.

Their first move was to address the issue of school lunch. They purchased the consumer-products division of Revolution Foods, a company known for providing healthy lunch options to schools. The attraction was a unique partnership that leveraged the Revolution Foods brand to address two sides of the school lunch experience: hot lunch and cold lunch.

Sheryl and Neil then purchased Plum Organics, a pioneer and leading provider of premium baby and toddler food. Then the team began enhancing their products. Plum Organics was previously an $800,000 frozen-baby-food business with two problems. Baby-food jars often break, making it a loss-leader category for retail stores and an inconvenience for parents. The frozen baby-food pouch partly solved this problem, but parents still had to defrost it. The second problem stemmed from store placement—parents just didn't look for baby food in the frozen-foods section. Sheryl and Neil searched for a solution that would make the baby food delicious and portable. They found an innovative European pouch with a flexible, childproof lid. The pouch held lightly cooked food, was more portable than others, and didn't need to be heated or defrosted. It transformed the baby-food industry, and within eighteen months, Plum Organics' sales had climbed to around $10 million and continue to skyrocket.

Although innovation was the root of their success, Sheryl also credits the foresight to invest in the right team. "We decided to invest in a professional management team up front who would have the skills and experience needed to meet our rapid growth," she says.

The other contributor to Nest Collective's success was its partnership approach with consumers. In 2010, Sheryl stepped out of her role as CEO to take on the title of Chief Mom, where she could continue to advocate for healthy eating. "Over 60 percent of the adults in America have young children. My goal was to help people understand that each time a parent feeds a healthy lunch to their kids, they are not only nourishing their own kids, they are also in a sense, becoming an activist and creating momentum for a healthy generation," she says.

Today, 3 percent of Revolution Foods' sales goes to provide lunch-line meals to underserved children. Revolution Foods and the Plum Organics lines are sold at Toys-R-Us, Whole Foods, and other regional and national outlets throughout the country. Recently, Sheryl and Neil were selected by *Bloomberg Businessweek* as two of "America's Most Promising Social Entrepreneurs" for making the concept of healthy food from high chair to the lunch box an everyday idea that matters.

As the business evolved, so did Sheryl's life. After four years at Nest Collective, she once again found an outlet for her advocacy as the executive director of the Center for Entrepreneurial Studies at Stanford University, where she now nurtures a new flock of emerging entrepreneurs.

"I see business as a way to better the world and make a difference, but I learned that unless your idea matters to a lot of people, your idea will stay just that: an idea," she says. "For me, it was about making healthy food indispensible to people. No matter what you set out to do, if you do it better than anyone else, then your enterprise *and* your social mission will matter."

Sharon's Story

Sharon Lechter Founder, Pay Your Family First Paradise Valley, Arizona		
Year Founded: 2008	Number of Employees: 4	Entrepreneurial Stage: 2
SmartGirls Strengths: Passion & Creativity		

Growing up as the daughter of small-business owners, Sharon Lechter learned firsthand the value of working hard for yourself and your family. After graduating in with honors in 1976 from Florida State University with a degree in accounting, she became one of the first women ever hired at her Big Eight accounting firm.

While working and raising a young family, her entrepreneurial spirit kicked into high gear. She started a woman's magazine, Wisconsin Woman, sold it, and then moved to publishing books. "As a mother of three fabulous kids, I was troubled by the fact that my children and their friends didn't like to read," she explains. "At about the same time, I had met the inventor of the first talking book. I realized this was a way to combine my passion as a parent with my business acumen, and so I joined forces with the founder to help him create Sight & Sound, which created a whole new category of children's educational tools."

Sight & Sound also launched Sharon's career in publishing and as a builder of companies. But it wasn't until 1992 when her eldest son went away to college and quickly acquired $2,500 in credit-card debt that her real entrepreneurial purpose emerged. "I was frustrated because I realized I hadn't taught him enough about how to manage his finances," she explains. "He had been with me when I used my credit cards, but he had never been with me when I paid them off. That was the day I decided to dedicate my life to the pursuit of financial education and financial literacy."

Her Vision-inspired Big Idea

Sharon's decision to focus on financial literacy led her to start the Rich Dad organization and co-author the book *Rich Dad, Poor Dad*—a parable that outlines how to achieve financial independence. The book made the top of the *New York Times* Best Sellers list in 2000 and led to fourteen other *Rich Dad* books. As the Rich Dad organization grew, Sharon's burning passion shifted toward the financial education of families, women, and young people: "I saw that our children are inheriting debt of unprecedented proportions, and, without adequate financial literacy education in the schools and the community, the mistakes of the past will be repeated in generations to come," she explains. "I wanted to create a company dedicated to empowering children and families to build prosperous futures through financial literacy education. I knew the experience needed to be fun and full of learning tools and opportunities."

In 2008, Sharon officially launched Pay Your Family First, a company dedicated to empowering entrepreneurs and building stronger communities through financial education and literacy. The goal was to concentrate on affordable and experiential products that would help women, families, and young people gain the skills and confidence to be financially successful. The company, now led by her son, has become the umbrella organization for a number of Sharon's newest brands and products, including YOUTHpreneur and the award-winning ThriveTime for Teens, both of which teach young people experiential lessons about money through reality game play. As Sharon states, "The best way to learn is through experience. Through game play, we can allow our children to 'stub their toes' while they play the game with fake money, instead of 'breaking their legs' with real money in the real world."

In 2008, Sharon was appointed by President Bush to serve on the first President's Advisory Council on Financial Literacy, helping to shape and advise both presidents Bush and Obama on financial literacy and education policy.

Sharon is also a national spokesperson for the American Institute of Certified Accountants and serves on the National CPAs Commission on Financial Literacy. She continues to reach and inspire people through her work as an author and as a collaborator with the Napoleon Hill Foundation, a nonprofit education institution dedicated to making the world a better place to live. Her book *Three Feet from Gold* and her recently annotated manuscript of Napoleon Hill's *Outwitting the Devil* are aimed at helping people turn obstacles into opportunities and live an abundant and rewarding life. Sharon also serves on the national boards of Childhelp and the Women Presidents Organization.

Learn more about Sharon at www.slechter.com/about.

These are just some of the amazing women running inspiring and important businesses. All of the women profiled in this book leveraged their unique feminine strengths to build successful businesses that are having a positive impact on their lives, their local communities, and the world. Their stories represent various stages of entrepreneurship (start-up to rapid growth) and provide practical and tangible advice for women who wish to launch their own successful enterprises.

The complete list of SmartGirls Way 100x100 Project entrepreneurs represents the diverse cross-section of women entrepreneurs today. SmartGirls entrepreneurs hail from over forty industries and range in age from eighteen to eighty-eight. They represent a breadth of ages and life situations including:

1. Self-starting young entrepreneurs under thirty who wish to work for themselves and champion social causes.
2. Life-shifting women aged thirty to forty who are balancing time and focus on their careers and family life.
3. Encore-entrepreneurs over fifty who are leaving successful business careers to start a new venture or follow a lifelong passion.

We hope they have energized you as you take your ViBI and turn it into a viable and thriving enterprise.

Notes

Foreword

1. Laura Jenner, Liz Mulligan-Ferry, and Rachel Soares, "2009 *Catalyst* Census: Fortune 500 Women Executive Officers and Top Earners," *Catalyst*, March 2010, http://www.catalyst.org/publication/358/2009-catalyst-census-fortune-500-women-executive-officers-and-top-earners.

Chapter 1

1. "U.S. Women in Business," *Catalyst*, August 2011, http://www.catalyst.org/publication/132/us-women-in-business.

2. See Linda Tarr-Whelan's formulation of the the "30% solution," in *Women Lead the Way: Your Guide to Stepping Up to Leadership and Changing the World* (San Francisco: Berrett-Koehler, 2009), 19. Tarr-Whelan cites the UN Division for advancement of Women, Fourth World Conference on Women, http://www.un.org/womenwatch/daw/beijing/platform/index.html; and Mayra Buvinic, Tine Lunde, and Nistha Sinha, "Investing in Gender Equality: Looking Ahead," *Economic Premise*, no. 22 (July 2010), http://siteresources.worldbank.org/INTPREMNET/Resources/EP22.pdf.

3. I. Elaine Allen, Amanda Elam, Nan Langowitz, and Monica Dean, "Global Entrepreneurship Monitor 2007 Report on Women and Entrepreneurship," Global Entrepreneurship Monitor, May 1, 2008, 1, http://www.gemconsortium.org/download/1316665137683/GEM%20GLOBAL%20Womens%20Report%202007.pdf.

4. Ibid.

5. J. McGrath Cohoon writes, "Women were much more likely than men—almost twice as likely—to secure their main funding from business partners." J. McGrath Cohoon, Vivek Wadhwa, and Lesa Mitchell, "The Anatomy of an Entrepreneur: Are Successful Women Entrepreneurs

Different from Men?" Kauffman, May 2010, http://www.kauffman.org/uploadedFiles/successful_women_entrepreneurs_5-10.pdf. Jeffrey Sohl, professor of entrepreneurship and director of the Center for Venture Research at the University of New Hampshire in Durham, asserts that "adding more women to the ranks of investors in startups...[is] key to helping female entrepreneurs since six years of survey data on angel investing found that women entrepreneurs were more likely to seek funding from groups with a higher number of female investors." (in Alexis Leondis, "Wall Street Women of Golden Seeds Give Cash to Female CEOs," Bloomberg, April 15, 2011, http://www.bloomberg.com/news/2011-04-15/wall-street-women-of-golden-seeds-use-angel-cash-to-cultivate-female-ceos.html).

6. See Erin Kepler and Scott Shane, "Are Male and Female Entrepreneurs Really That Different?" Small Business Association Office of Advocacy, September 2007, http://archive.sba.gov/advo/research/rs309tot.pdf, and Jodyanne Kirkwood, "Is a Lack of Self-Confidence Hindering Women Entrepreneurs?" *International Journal of Gender and Entrepreneurship* 1, no. 2 (2009): 118–33.

7. "Left to its own devices, the [E]arth is a sustainable system. As we continue to learn, however, the accumulated impacts of human activity over the past two centuries are now threatening our continued well-being." NaturalStep.org, http://www.naturalstep.org/the-system-conditions.

8. Daniel Quinn, *Ishmael: An Adventure of the Mind and Spirit* (New York: Bantam, 1995).

9. Jonathon Porritt, in discussion with the author, Seattle, May 2009. See also *Capitalism as if the World Matters* (London: Earthscan, 2005).

10. Paul Hawken, *The Ecology of Commerce: A Declaration of Sustainability* (New York: Harper Business, 1993), quoted by *Publisher's Weekly* on Amazon.com/Ecology-Commerce-Declaration-Sustainability/dp/0887307043.

11. Riane Eisler, *The Real Wealth of Nations* (San Francisco: Berrett-Koehler, 2008), Kindle edition. See esp. Chapter 3, 580–827.

12. Anthony Faiola, Ellen Nakashima, and Jill Drew, "The Crash: What Went Wrong, Part 1: Risk and Regulation," *Washington Post*,

October 15, 2008, http://www.washingtonpost.com/wp-dyn/content/article/2008/10/14/AR2008101403343_pf.html.

13. See Heather Boushey, "The New Breadwinners," http://www.shriverreport.com/awn/economy.php, distilled from Maria Shriver and the Center for American Progress, *The Shriver Report: A Woman's Nation Changes Everything*, edited by Heather Boushey and Ann O'Leary (Washington, D.C.: Center for American Progress, 2009).

14. David R. Francis, "Why Do Women Outnumber Men in College?" National Bureau of Economic Research, January 2007, http://www.nber.org/digest/jan07/w12139.html.

15. Barbara Kellerman, "The Abiding Tyranny of the Male Leadership Model—A Manifesto," *Harvard Business Review Blog*, April 27, 2010, http://blogs.hbr.org/imagining-the-future-of-leadership/2010/04/the-abiding-tyranny-of-the-mal.html.

16. Claudio Sanchez, interview with Nathan Bell of the U.S. Council of Graduate Schools, "Women Outnumber Men Earning Doctoral Degrees," *Morning Edition*, National Public Radio, September 15, 2010.

17. David Getz, "Men's and Women's Earnings for States and Metropolitan Statistical Areas: 2009," American Community Survey Briefs, U.S. Census, September 2010, http://www.census.gov/prod/2010pubs/acsbr09-3.pdf. See also 2009 U.S. Census findings as reported by the Associated Press, "Census Says Women Equal to Men in Advanced Degrees, Yet They Still Lag Behind Men in Pay," April 20, 2010, http://www.oregonlive.com/politics/index.ssf/2010/04/census_says_women_equal_to_men.html.

18. Online Women in Politics, "Statistics," updated April 2009, http://www.onlinewomeninpolitics.org/statistics.htm.

19. Tarr-Whelan, "Less than 3% of CEOs are Women," in *Women Lead the Way*, 19.

20. Interview with Ilene Lang of *Catalyst*, "Only 3% of CEOs Are Women," CNBC Moneywatch, December 9, 2009, http:// www.moneywatch.bnet.com/career-advice/video/only-3-of-ceos-are-women/371879.

21. Louann Brizendine, *The Female Brain* (New York: Morgan Road Books, 2006), 17–23.

22. Gerda Lerner, *The Creation of Patriarchy* (New York: Oxford University Press, 1986), referenced in Michael C. Kearl, "Gender and Society," Trinity University website, accessed August 24, 2011, http://www.trinity.edu/~mkearl/gender.html.

23. Tarr-Whelan, *Women Lead the Way*, 19.

24. American Express OPEN, "The American Express OPEN State of Women-Owned Businesses Report: A Summary of Important Trends, 1997–2011," March 30, 2011, http://media.nucleus.naprojects.com/pdf/WomanReport_FINAL.pdf.

Chapter 2

1. Kearl, "Gender and Society."

Chapter 3

1. Allen et al., "Global Entrepreneurship Monitor 2007 Report."

Chapter 4

1. "INTEGRITY. n. 1: firm adherence to a code of especially moral or artistic values : INCORRUPTIBILITY 2: an unimpaired condition : SOUNDNESS 3: the quality or state of being complete or undivided : COMPLETENESS." From *Merriam-Webster* online, http://www.merriam-webster.com/dictionary/integrity.

2. "Of the nearly $125 million in completed loans Kiva has funded, 98.91 percent of them have been repaid by the end of the loan's term." Kiva website, "About Us," accessed August 25, 2011, http://www.kiva.org/about.

3. Women's Philanthropy Institute at the Center on Philanthropy at Indiana University, "WomenGive 2010 Part 2: Causes Women Support: New Research About Women and Giving," December 2010, http://www.philanthropy.iupui.edu/womengive/docs/CausesWomenSupport.pdf.

4. Deniz S. Ones and Chockalingam Viswesvaran, "Gender, Age, and Race Differences on Overt Integrity Tests: Results Across Four Large-Scale Job Applicant Datasets," *Journal of Applied Psychology* 83, no. 1 (1998): 35–42.

5. Malcolm Gladwell, *Blink* (New York: Little, Brown and Company, 2005), 23.

6. "The circuits for social and verbal connections are naturally hard-wired in the female brain." Brizendine, *The Female Brain*, 36.

7. Y. W. Shin et al. "Sex Differences in the Corpus Callosum: Diffusion Tensor Imaging Study," *Neuroreport* 16, no. 8 (2005): 795–98.

8. Allen et al., "Global Entrepreneurship Monitor 2007 Report."

9. "There was a positive correlation between self-report measures of self-esteem, but the relationship was both stronger and more consistent for women than for men." John Baer and James C. Kaufman, "Gender Differences in Creativity," *Journal of Creative Behavior* 42, no. 2 (2008): 75–105, http://users.rider.edu/~baer/BaerKaufmanGenderDifferences.pdf.

10. K. R. G. Nair and Anu Panday, "Characteristics of Entrepreneurs: An Empirical Analysis," *Journal of Enterpreneurship* 15, no. 1 (2006): 47–61.

11. "PASSION. n. 4 b: intense, driving, or overmastering feeling or conviction c: an outbreak of anger 5 a: ardent affection : LOVE b: a strong liking or desire for or devotion to some activity, object, or concept." From *Merriam-Webster* online, http://www.merriam-webster.com/dictionary/passion.

12. Tarr-Whelan, *Women Lead the Way*, 96.

13. Brian K. Lebowitz and Michael F. Brown, "Sex Differences in Spatial Search and Pattern Learning in the Rat," *Psychobiology* 3 (1999): 364–71, http://www.pigeon.psy.tufts.edu/ccs/pubs/files/2822-LebowirzBrown1999.pdf.

14. "Being employed and having a social network that includes other entrepreneurs are stronger predictors of women's entrepreneurship than educational attainment or household income." Allen et al., "Global Entrepreneurship Monitor 2007 Report," 4.

15. Auren Hoffman, "The Social Media Gender Gap," *Business Week*, May 19, 2008, http://www.businessweek.com/technology/content/may2008/tc20080516_580743.htm.

16. See the Infomania Experiment for HP conducted by Glenn Wilson in 2005. In keeping with the notion that women are better at

multitasking, the study demonstrated that females were far better than males at handling distraction. http://www.drglennwilson.com/Infomania_experiment_for_HP.doc.

17. B. R. Criss, "Gender Differences in Multitasking," National Undergraduate Research Clearing House 9 (2006), http://www.webclearinghouse.net/volume/9/CRISS-GenderDiff.php.

Chapter 6

1. Steven Covey's "Habit 4," in *The Seven Habits of Highly Effective People* (New York: Simon and Schuster, 1989), 204–34.

2. Allen et al., "Global Entrepreneurship Monitor 2007 Report," 4.

3. Christine Percheski, "Opting Out? Cohort Differences in Professional Women's Employment Rates from 1960 to 2005," *American Sociological Review* 73, no. 3 (June 2008), 497–517. See further discussion of Percheski's groundbreaking work in Jackie Cooper's "Opting Out Revolution a Myth: Study Shows Steep Employment Gains for Women, Mothers," American Sociological Association, June 2008, http://www.eurekalert.org/pub_releases/2008-06/asa-oor061008.php: "Despite anecdotal reports of successful working women returning to the home to assume child care responsibilities, less than 8 percent of professional women born since 1956 leave the workforce for a year or more during their prime childbearing years, according to the study. Percheski's research shows that the number of women with young children who work full-time year-round has increased steadily,... Not only are more women with children working, but Percheski's research shows a trend of women working longer hours. 'Contrary to an opt-out revolution, professional women—including mothers of young children—are working more than ever,' said Percheski. 'Despite this increase in women's employment, we can not [sic] assume that combining professional work and family life is easy for most women. Indeed, many working women successfully combine these roles by making great personal sacrifices, including curtailing their sleep, civic involvement or leisure time."

4. See the new annotated version of Napoleon Hill's *Outwitting the Devil* (originally published in 1938) edited by Sharon Lechter, a member of the Napoleon Hill Foundation. *Outwitting the Devil: The Secret*

to Freedom and Success (New York: Sterling, 2011), http://www.azshare.info/e-books/27243-napoleon-hill-outwitting-the-devil.html.

5. Allen et al., "Global Entrepreneurship Monitor 2007 Report," 1.

6. Michael Lechter, *OPM: Other People's Money: How to Attract Other People's Money for Your Investments—the Ultimate Leverage* (New York: Time Warner Books, 2005). Michael is Sharon Lechter's husband and business partner.

7. Another informative book on the topic of venture capital is Brad Feld and Jason Mendelson's *Venture Deals: Be Smarter than Your Lawyer and Venture Capitalist* (Hoboken, NJ: Wiley Publishing, 2011).

8. For a business-plan template by the Small Business Association, go to http://web.sba.gov/busplantemplate/BizPlanStart.cfm.

9. For a business-plan nondisclosure agreement: http://www.legalzoom.com/legalforms/business-plan-nondisclosure-agreement.html.

10. To learn how to apply for trademarks: http://www.uspto.gov.

11. A primer on intellectual-property protection: http://www.uspto.gov/trademarks/basics/index.jsp.

12. Examples of crowd-funding: http://www.kickstarter.com, http://www.indiegogo.com.

13. Peer-to-peer lending site examples: http://www.microventures.com, https://www.profounder.com, http://www.prosper.com.

14. For more information on Small Business Administration loans, see http://www.sba.gov/aboutsba/history/index.html and http://www.sba.gov/aboutsba/sbaprograms/onlinewbc/index.html.

15. Review of ERISA and IRS requirements is critical for any venture.

16. Mass Challenge, http://masschallenge.org.

17. Make Mine a Million $ Business, http://www.makemineamillion.org.

18. See the Eileen Fischer Foundation's Women-Owned Business Grants, http://www.eileenfisher.com/EileenFisherCompany/CompanyGeneralContentPages/SocialConciousness/Supporting_Women.jsp?bmLocale=en_US.

19. TechStars, http://www.techstars.org/network.

20. Cambridge Innovation Center, http://www.cictr.com.

21. Rainier Valley Community Development Fund, http://www.rvcdf.org/what_we_offer_business.php.

22. Golden Seeds, http://www.goldenseeds.com/investors/overview.

23. Allen et al., "Global Entrepreneurship Monitor 2007 Report," 1.

Chapter 7

1. A 2009 study from the Institute for Employment Research in Nuremberg, Germany, showed that personality traits such as "agreeableness" were not beneficial in the workplace: "For women, it does not pay to be nice: 'Alpha females' earn £40,000 more in their lifetime," July 14, 2009, http://www.dailymail.co.uk/femail/article-1199367/Women-act-like-men-earn-40-000-feminine-colleagues-Essex-University-study-shows.html#ixzz1N6A10CR7.

2. "Poor communication contributes to a high failure rate," according to T. J. Larkin and Sandar Larkin in "Communicating Big Change using Small Communication," (2004), 8, http://www.larkin.biz/documents/Comm_Big_Change-Larkin.pdf.

Chapter 9

1. 100×100 Project: a SmartGirls Way initiative, www.SmartGirlsWay.com.

Bibliography & Resources

Allen, I. Elaine, et al. "The Global Entrepreneurship Monitor 2007 Report on Women and Entrepreneurship." Global Entrepreneurship Monitor. 2008. http://www.gemconsortium.org/about.aspx?page=special_topic_women.

American Express OPEN. "The American Express OPEN State of Women-Owned Businesses Report." March 30, 2011. http://www.openforum.com/idea-hub/topics/innovation/article/the-american-express-open-state-of-women-owned-businesses-report-american-express-open?intlink=us-openf-nav-gallery.

Baer, John, and James C. Kaufman. "Gender Differences in Creativity." *The Journal of Creative Behavior* 42, 2 (2008): 75–105. http://www.psychology.csub.edu/facultyStaff/Kauffman Baer2008.pdf.

Becker-Blease, John R. "Do Women-Owned Businesses Have Equal Access to Angel Capital?" *Journal of Business Venturing*. 2007. http://www.wsbe.unh.edu/Centers_CVR/publications.cfm.

Boushey, Heather. "The New Breadwinners." Distilled from Maria Shriver and the Center for American Progress, *The Shriver Report: A Woman's Nation Changes Everything*. Edited by Heather Boushey and Ann O'Leary. Washington, D.C.: Center for American Progress, 2009. http://www.shriverreport.com/awn/economy.php

Brizendine, Louann. *The Female Brain*. New York: Morgan Road Books, 2006.

Cohoon, J. McGrath, Vivek Wadhwa, and Lesa Mitchell. *The Anatomy of an Entrepreneur: Are Successful Women Entrepreneurs Different from Men?* Ewing Marion Kauffman Foundation, 2010.

Cooper, Jackie. "Opting Out Revolution a Myth: Study Shows Steep Employment Gains for Women, Mothers." American Sociological Association. June 2008. http://www.eurekalert.org/pub_releases/2008-06/asa-oor061008.php.

Covey, Stephen. *The Seven Habits of Highly Effective People.* New York: Simon and Schuster, 1989.

Criss, B. R. "Gender Differences in Multitasking." National Undergraduate Research Clearing House, 9 (2006). http://www.webclearinghouse.net/volume/9/CRISS-GenderDiff.php.

Daily Mail Online. "For Women, It Does Not Pay to Be Nice: 'Alpha Females' Earn £40,000 More in Their Lifetime." July 14, 2009. http://www.dailymail.co.uk/femail/article-1199367/Women-act-like-men-earn-40-000-feminine-colleagues-Essex-University-study-shows.html.

Eisler, Riane. *The Real Wealth of Nations: Creating a Caring Economics.* San Francisco: Berrett-Koehler Publishers, 2008. Kindle edition.

Faiola, Anthony, Ellen Nakashima, and Jill Drew. "The Crash: What Went Wrong, Part 1: Risk and Regulation." *Washington Post*, October 15, 2008. http://www.washingtonpost.com/wpdyn/content/article/2008/10/14/AR2008101403343.html.

Feld, Brad, and Jason Mendelson. *Venture Deals: Be Smarter than Your Lawyer and Venture Capitalist.* Hoboken, NJ: Wiley Publishing, 2011.

Francis, David R. "Why Do Women Outnumber Men in College?" National Bureau of Economic Research, January 2007. http://www.nber.org/digest/jan07/w12139.html.

Getz, David. "Men's and Women's Earnings for States and Metropolitan Statistical Areas." *Community Briefs*, September 2010. U.S. Census. http://www.census.gov/prod/2010pubs/acsbr09-3.pdf.

Gladwell, Malcolm. *Blink.* New York: Little, Brown and Company, 2005.

Hawken, Paul. *The Ecology of Commerce: A Declaration of Sustainability.* New York: Harper Business, 1993.

Hill, Napoleon. *Think and Grow Rich.* 1937. http://www.archive.org/details/Think_and_Grow_Rich.

———. *Outwitting the Devil: The Secret to Freedom and Success*. Edited by Sharon Lechter. New York: Sterling, 2011. http://www.azshare.info/e-books/27243-napoleon-hill-outwitting-the-devil.html.

Hoffman, Auren. "The Social Media Gender Gap." *Business Week*, May 19, 2008, http://www.businessweek.com/technology/content/may2008/tc20080516_580743.htm.

Investopedia Website. www.investopedia.com/#axzz1Vuj6oz99.

Jenner, Laura, Liz Mulligan-Ferry, and Rachel Soares. "2009 Catalyst Census: Fortune 500 Women Executive Officers and Top Earners." *Catalyst*, March 2010. http://www.catalyst.org/publication/358/2009-catalyst-census-fortune-500-women-executive-officers-and-top-earners.

Kearl, Michael C. "Gender and Society." Trinity University Website. Accessed August 24, 2011. http://www.trinity.edu/~mkearl/gender.html.

Kellerman, Barbara. "The Abiding Tyranny of the Male Leadership Model—A Manifesto." *Harvard Business Review Blog*. April 27, 2010. http://blogs.hbr.org/imagining-the-future-of-leadership/2010/04/the-abiding-tyranny-of-the-mal.html.

Kepler, Erin, and Scott Shane. "Are Male and Female Entrepreneurs Really that Different?" Small Business Association Office of Advocacy. 2007. http://archive.sba.gov/advo/research/rs309tot.pdf.

Kirkwood, Jodyanne. "Is a Lack of Self-Confidence Hindering Women Entrepreneurs?" *International Journal of Gender and Entrepreneurship* 1, no. 2 (2009): 118–33. http://www.emeraldinsight.com/Insight/ViewContentServlet?contentType=Article&Filename=/published/emeraldfulltextarticle/pdf/ijge-jan-2009-0001_rtc_cl_final.pdf

Kiva website. "About Us." Accessed August 25, 2011. http://www.kiva.org/about.

Lang, Ilene. "Only 3% of CEOs are Women." CNBC Moneywatch. December 9, 2009. http://www.moneywatch.bnet.com/career-advice/video/only-3-of-ceos-are-women/371879/?tag=content;col1.

Larkin, T. J., and Sandra Larkin. "Communicating Big Change using Small Communication." 2004. http://www.larkin.biz/documents/Comm_Big_Change-Larkin.pdf.

Lebowitz, Brian K., and Michael F. Brown. "Sex Differences in Spatial Search and Pattern Learning in the Rat." *Psychobiology* 27, no. 3 (1999): 364–71. http://www.pigeon.psy.tufts.edu/ccs/pubs/files/2822-LebowirzBrown1999.pdf.

Lechter, Michael. *OPM: Other People's Money: How to Attract Other People's Money for Your Investments—the Ultimate Leverage*. New York: Time Warner Books, 2005.

Leondis, Alexis. "Wall Street Women of Golden Seeds Give Cash to Female CEOs." *Bloomberg*. April 15, 2011.

Lerner, Gerda. *The Creation of Patriarchy*. New York: Oxford University Press, 1986.

Nair, K. R. G., and Anu Panday. "Characteristics of Entrepreneurs: An Empirical Analysis." *Journal of Entrepreneurship* 15, no. 1 (2006): 47–61.

NaturalStep.org. "The Four System Conditions." http://www.naturalstep.org/en/the-system-conditions.

Ones, Deniz S., and Chockalingam Viswesvaran. "Gender, Age, and Race Differences on Overt Integrity Tests: Results Across Four Large-Scale Job Applicant Datasets." *Journal of Applied Psychology* 83, no. 1 (1998): 35–42.

Online Women in Politics. "Statistics." Updated April 2009. http://www.onlinewomeninpolitics.org/statistics.htm.

Percheski, Christine. "Opting Out? Cohort Differences in Professional Women's Employment Rates from 1960 to 2005." *American Sociological Review* 73, no. 3 (June 2008): 497–517.

Porritt, Jonathon. *Capitalism as if the World Matters*. London: Earthscan, 2005.

Quinn, Daniel. *Ishmael: An Adventure of the Mind and Spirit*. New York: Bantam, 1995.

Sanchez, Claudio. Interview with Nathan Bell of the U.S. Council of Graduate Schools. "Women Outnumber Men Earning Doctoral Degrees." *Morning Edition*. National Public Radio. September 15, 2010.

Shin, Y. W., et al. "Sex Differences in the Corpus Callosum: Diffusion Tensor Imaging Study." *Neuroreport* 16, no. 8 (2005): 795–98. http://journals.lww.com/neuroreport/pages/articleviewer.aspx?year=2005&issue=05310&article=00003&type=abstract.

Tarr-Whelan, Linda. *Women Lead the Way: Your Guide to Stepping Up to Leadership and Changing the World*. San Francisco: Berrett-Koehler, 2009.

U.S. Census 2009. Reported by the *Associated Press*. April 20, 2010. http://www.oregonlive.com/politics/index.ssf/2010/04/census_says_women_equal_to_men.html.

"U.S. Women in Business." *Catalyst*. August 2011. http://www.catalyst.org/publication/132/us-women-in-business.

Wilson, Glenn. "Infomania Experiment for HP." 2005. http://www.drglennwilson.com/Infomania_experiment_for_HP.doc.

Women's Philanthropy Institute at the Center on Philanthropy at Indiana University. "WomenGive 2010 Part 2: Causes Women Support, New Research About Women and Giving, December." December 2010. http://www.philanthropy.iupui.edu/womengive/docs/CausesWomenSupport.pdf.

Additional Works Consulted

Bennett, Jessica, and Jesse Ellison. "Women Will Rule the World: Men Were the Main Victims of the Recession. The Recovery Will Be Female." *Newsweek*: TheDailyBeast.com. July 5, 2010. http://www.thedailybeast.com/newsweek/2010/07/06/women-will-rule-the-world.html.

Blank, Rebecca M. *Women-Owned Business in the 21st Century*. U.S. Department of Commerce and Economics and Statistics Administration. October 2010. http://www.esa.doc.gov/sites/default/files/reports/documents/women-owned-businesses.pdf.

Blank, Steve. "Boys Rules, Girls Lose—Women at Work." FastCompany.com. Aug 31, 2010. http://www.fastcompany.com/1685949/boys-rules-girls-lose-women-at-work.

Brush, Candida, et al. "Cash and the Woman-Owned Business," Harvard Business School Working Knowledge. September 13, 2004. http://hbswk.hbs.edu/cgi-bin/print?id=4365.

Colligan, Victoria. "A Better Alternative for Women-Owned Business." Forbes.com, September 1, 2009. http://www.forbes.com/2009/09/01/women-owned-business-launch-forbes-woman-entrepreneurs-lifestyle.html.

Kim, Jane J. "As Prosper Gets the Greenlight, A Comeback for Peer-to-Peer Lenders?" *Wall Street Journal, The Wallet Blog*. July 14, 2009. http://blogs.wsj.com/wallet/2009/07/14/as-prosper-gets-the-greenlight-a-comeback-for-peer-to-peer-lenders.

National Women's Business Council. "SBA Lending Improves to Women Owned Businesses." April 27, 2004. http://www.nwbc.gov/idc/groups/public/documents/nwbc/press_release052704.pdf

Rampel, Catherine. "Women Now a Majority in American Workplaces." *New York Times,* February 6, 2010. http://www.nytimes.com/2010/02/06/business/economy/06women.html.

Rosenthal, Bruce. "Survey Finds Women Business Owners are Philanthropic Leaders." AllBusiness.com. http://www.allbusiness.com/management/816113-1.html.

Rosin, Hanna. "The End of Men." *The Atlantic.* July/August, 2010. http://www.theatlantic.com/magazine/archive/2010/07/the-end-of-men/8135/

Smith, Charles Hugh. "Does America's New Economy Favor Women?" *Daily Finance.* June 16, 2010. http://www.dailyfinance.com/2010/06/16/does-americas-new-economy-favor-women.

Wilson, Fred. "One Thing You Don't Need to Be an Entrepreneur: A College Education." *A VC: Musings of a VC in New York Blog.* February 26, 2009. http://www.avc.com/a_vc/2009/02/one-thing-you-dont-need-to-be-an-entrepreneur-a-college-degree.html

Zhang Yang, Alison. "Women in the New Economy." *The Yale Herald.* March 23, 2001. http://www.yaleherald.com/archive/xxxi/2001.03.23/features/exclusive.html

Online Resources

Business Strategy and Protection

Business Plan

Small Business Association. http://web.sba.gov/busplantemplate/BizPlanStart.cfm

Intellectual-Property Protection, Trademarks, and Patents

United States Patent and Trademark Office. http://www.uspto.gov/trademarks/basics/index.jsp

Nondisclosure Agreement

Legal Zoom. http://www.legalzoom.com

Funding

Angel Investment

Golden Seeds. http://www.goldenseeds.com/investors/overview

Micro-Financing and Peer-to-Peer Lending

IndieGoGo. http://www.indiegogo.com

Kick Starter. http://www.kickstarter.com

MicroVentures. http://www.microventures.com

Profounder. https://www.profounder.com

Grants and Loans

Eileen Fischer Foundation. http://www.eileenfisher.com/EileenFisherCompany/CompanyGeneralContentPages/SocialConciousness/Supporting_Women.jsp?bmLocale=en_US

Make Mine a Million $ Business. http://www.makemineamillion.org

Mass Challenge.com. http://masschallenge.org

Rainier Valley Community Development Fund. http://www.rvcdf.org/what_we_offer_business.php

Small Business Administration. http://www.sba.gov/aboutsba/history/index.html and http://www.sba.gov/aboutsba/sbaprograms/onlinewbc/index.html

Incubators

Techstars. http://www.techstars.org/network

Cambridge Innovation Center. http://www.cictr.com

GLOSSARY

80/20 Principle: the assertion that approximately 80 percent of the effects come from 20 percent of the causes, or that 80 percent of the impact comes from 20 percent of the efforts

action element: the part of your business plan in which you create a concrete set of steps to move from dreaming and exploring to creating and launching

angel investors: committed individuals who invest personal capital in exchange for convertible debt or equity

bootstrapping: funding your business through your existing job or personal savings

Champions: friends, financiers, suppliers, business partners, supporters, and others who provide more than general support by enthusiastically promoting you and your business; may include your advisory board and investors, but also early adopters of your business service or product

Cheerleaders: those whose opinions and word of mouth can make or break your business; often your best customers and early adopters of your product, service, or solution

Collaborators: those you entrust to help you actualize your vision and grow your business; employees or business partners, domestic partners, parents, children, and child-care providers; those who are fundamental to your overall work/life balance

competitive matrix: a tool that helps you compare your product or service to those of your competitors to identify your unique, competitive advantage

Creativity: to explore the outer limits of ideas, make new connections and new things, and think of new ideas; in the context of the SmartGirls Way, creating a visual picture of how your business will look when it is thriving, and uncovering solutions, opportunities, and breakthroughs on the path to that success

critical priorities: the issues and opportunities that are most critical to the success of your business

crowd-funding: an online peer-to-peer contribution model that helps you find a community of small contributors to fund your business without the traditional risks of financing

Curiosity: a desire to know, an inquisitive interest leading to inquiry; in the context of the SmartGirls Way, the ability to understand how your **ViBI** fits in the world and seeking out those ideas that are similar to your own

early-stage capital: raising capital to support entry into the marketplace and see your company through its early research, development, and growth

elevator pitch: a brief marketing pitch, ideally short enough to be communicated in the length of an elevator ride, used to engage potential investors, customers, or partners in conversation about your business; also called a "**short story**"

Emotional Intelligence (EI) quotient: the perceived ability to identify, assess, and manage the emotions of oneself, of others, and of groups

entrepreneurs: people with **ViBIs** who use Intuition, Creativity, and personal Integrity to build thriving businesses and who take ultimate accountability for the success of their businesses

equity: the quantified value of your company assets

eureka moment: the moment when, like the famous Greek philosopher Archimedes, an individual discovers a breakthrough idea

executive summary: outlines the contents of your business plan in such a way that an investor can quickly understand your business model, what you are planning to deliver to the marketplace, why your solution is relevant to your customers, how you plan to operate and market your business, expected revenue, costs, profit and loss, and your timeline for reaching your goals within the next three to five years

external strengths: strengths that tend to be visible to the external world; less of a reflection of how you feel about your vision and more a measure of your general competence, preference, and comfort in how you bring that vision to life; also called **optimizer strengths**. See also **Passion, Curiosity, Weaving**

FOCUS process: stands for *Find your relevancy, Organize and Commit to action, Underwrite yourself, and Start!*; the action element of your business plan that outlines the thinking and actions required to turn your **ViBI** into a business

FUD factor: *Fear, Uncertainty, and Doubt*; essentially a common term for "appealing to your fears"

grants: company grants and contests awarded by government organizations, nonprofits, and/or foundations

Great Recession: sometimes referred to as the "mancession," the economic downturn of the 2000s in the United States that resulted in, for the first time, women outnumbering men as primary breadwinners within families

growth capital: capital needed for the rapid expansion and scaling of your company as your company matures and your customer base expands

incubator: programs designed to accelerate the successful inception and evolution of entrepreneurial companies through an array of business-support resources and services

Integrity: honest and unimpaired adherence to our moral principles; in the context of the SmartGirls Way, the strength that addresses the impact and actions of your business on others (community, family, the world) in terms of justice, fairness, and equity

internal strengths: strengths that are typically a reflection of what goes on within you and play a critical role in assessing your desire to invest effort, money, intelligence, time, and other resources that turn your idea or vision into a business. *See also* **Integrity, Intuition, Creativity**

Intuition: the "adaptive unconscious"; the mental process that works rapidly and automatically from relatively little information to come to a conclusion or make decisions; in the context of the SmartGirls Way, the strength that helps us take in the slices of information we receive and relate them to a person, information, or situation

joint venture: a business agreement in which two or more parties agree to develop, for a finite time, a new entity and new assets by contributing equity. *See also* **longer-term strategic alliance**

legacy thinking: the generally accepted and sometimes invisible attitudes, practices, and policies inherent in an established culture, business, or society; invisible or unexamined norms

leverage point: the point within a larger system at which a small shift in one thing can produce a big change in everything

longer-term strategic alliance: where two organizations share initiatives and resources to build a mutually advantageous competitive advantage

micro-lending: also known as "**social lending**" or "**peer-to-peer lending**"; individuals borrow and lend money without an intermediary financial institution

Myers-Briggs Type Indicator (MBTI): a psychometric questionnaire designed to measure psychological preferences in how people perceive the world and make decisions

next economy: economic vitality as understood from the perspective of a healthy planet and a viable and thriving future; built on principles that embrace the ecosystem that supports us, our responsibility to each other, and our legacy to future generations

nondisclosure agreement (NDA): also called a *confidentiality agreement*; a legal document you ask potential investors, employees, or other stakeholders to sign before sharing confidential details regarding your idea or business plan; creates a confidential relationship between the parties to protect any type of confidential and proprietary information or trade secrets, including intellectual property

Opportunities: in the context of a **SWOT analysis**, the external elements and chances that help you grow your business

optimizer strengths: strengths that tend to be visible to the external world; less of a reflection of how you feel about your vision and more a measure of your general competence, preference, and comfort in how you bring that vision to life; also called **external strengths**. *See also* **Passion, Curiosity, Weaving**

optimizing: how well you are using any given strength, in a considered and intentional manner, to its fullest and best use

Passion: an emotion or the visible expression of a strong, barely controllable enthusiasm; in the context of the SmartGirls Way, the emotion that gives energy, and when used and responded to in tandem with **optimizer strengths**, can be the most important leverage point for your business

peer-to-peer lending: also known as "**social lending**" or "**micro-lending**"; individuals borrow and lend money without an intermediary financial institution

personal loans: negotiating a monthly rate with interest terms against a personal line of credit or asset

primary stakeholders: the most important people to the success of your business; can include customers, vendors, partners, staff, members of the media, government and legal decision makers, investors—anyone who is associated with or has a perception of your brand or business and whose decisions or opinions have a significant impact on your business

private equity partners: groups that take a private equity stake in small- and middle-market companies looking to drive steady growth and profitability; often take on a senior management or board-level role to ensure control and growth

quick wins: what are sometimes called "low-hanging fruit"; those initial milestones and accomplishments that define your initial success in reaching your business goals

radical honesty: putting the entire truth—what you see, what you sense, and the questions you have—on the table in a direct and no-nonsense way

RASI chart: stands for *Responsibility, Accountability, Support, and Inform;* a tool to help create a clarity of control and clear accountability

retirement-fund financing: using your existing IRA or 401(k) retirement plan to fund your business

SCAN process: stands for *See, Connect, Analyze, and Nest*; the research and planning phase that will help you build your business plan in an informed way, analyze and understand how your business fits into the world, and measure the context and community in which your customer and your **ViBI** reside

scarcity mentality: the tendency to look at a situation and see what is lacking or missing, instead of seeing abundance and possibility; having a win/lose outlook instead of a win-win outlook

secondary stakeholders: those who influence your primary stakeholders or to whom your primary stakeholders are responsible

security: a negotiable or fluctuating value of a piece (or commodity) of your company; issued as a financial certificate in the form of a stock, fund, or bond that someone other than you may own; its involvement can entail severe legal ramifications unless the offering fits within very specific exemptions to both federal and state security laws

sexism: the application of the belief or attitude that there are characteristics implicit to one's gender that indirectly (and stereotypically) affect one's abilities

short story: commonly known as the "**elevator pitch**"; a brief marketing pitch, ideally short enough to be communicated in the length of an elevator ride, used to engage potential investors, customers, or partners in conversation about your business

Small Business Administration loans: loans provided by banks for small businesses where the government acts as guarantor

Small Business Association (SBA): government-funded association supporting small businesses across the United States via advocacy and services

SmartGirls Mirror: a diagnostic that tests your day-to-day optimization of six specific feminine characteristics and illuminates your strongest behaviors against your **ViBI**

SmartGirls Way Methodology: a series of natural and logical steps that break the entrepreneurial process down into three practical phases and put you in control of your business growth

Stakeholder Map: a visual representation of the network of relationships between (and among) you and your **primary** and **secondary stakeholders**; a tool to help you identify and then engage with stakeholders

stakeholders: people who have some kind of interest or concern in your business; can be **primary stakeholders** or **secondary stakeholders**

start-up capital: often called "seed funding"; the amount of money required to develop and start your business and see it through its very early stages

Strengths: in the context of a **SWOT analysis**, the internal attributes and characteristics of your business that give you a competitive advantage

sustainability: the core concept that human society survives only because of the ecosystem that supports our basic needs; acting in a sustainable model means meeting the needs of today's society without making it impossible for future generations to also enjoy life on Planet Earth

sustainable business: a business that has no net (negative) impact on the global or local environment, community, society, or economy; in the higher sense, a business that is designed to create

sweat equity: giving equity in your company in exchange for work, talent, and products developed for the company

SWOT analysis: a tool that helps you compare your product or service to those of your competitors to identify your unique competitive advantage by exploring your **Strengths, Weaknesses, Opportunities,** and **Threats**

Threats: in the context of a **SWOT analysis**, the external elements that can cause trouble for your business

THRIVE process: stands for *Trust, Honesty, Responsibility, Intention, Values, and Empowerment*; the five core principles critical to scaling and operating successful business

tranches: the individual slices or portions of your company's valuation; sometimes referred to as *funding rounds*

triple bottom line: bottom-line profit principle related to sustainability that takes into account the impact on people, profit, and planet

value chain: the process for organizing the steps your product or services go through from creation to delivery in order to ensure you deliver maximum value for both your business and your customer

value proposition: a short, concise statement explaining what differentiates your product or service; helps you identify and articulate what you want your business to be known for

venture-capital (VC) groups: a group or entity that takes a stake in your business with the goal to exponentially grow a company; beyond cash, VCs often provide other expertise or resources the entrepreneur needs

Vision-inspired Big Idea (ViBI): an entrepreneurial idea that is fueled by a sense of integrity and a passion to see a critical need or opportunity addressed

visual pitch: a presentation you give to engage potential investors; should be visually engaging and concisely explain your executive summary, your financial plan, key trends and decision-making benchmarks, and a demonstration or example of your product or service

Weaknesses: in the context of a **SWOT analysis**, the internal limitations or obstacles that place you at a disadvantage

Weaving: a collective strength that uses networking, community building, listening, and social sensitivity skills, as well as communication and multitasking abilities; in the context of the SmartGirls Way, the ability to see patterns of connections and visualize constellations of ideas, people, and markets around business ideas

word cloud: word-association exercise that helps you to generate a group of dominant words that can aid in articulating your idea to the outside world, as well as helping you to shape a value proposition for your **ViBI**

INDEX

100×100 Project, 90, 137, 140–41, 164
30% solution, 7
401(k), funding your business with, 102–03
80%20 Shoes, 24, 51–52, 144–46
80/20 Principle, 51
action: committing to, 85–86; meeting passion, 11–12
Africa Direct, 19–20, 81–82, 126, 141–43
Allen, Stephanie, 88, 55–56, 155–57
AllVoices.com, 111–12, 150–51
American Institute of CPAs' Commission on Financial Literacy, 90
amplifier strengths. *See* external strengths
angel investment groups, 106
Bainbridge Graduate Institute, 84
balance, work/life, 35, 26–27: myth of conflict in, 91; trade-offs in, 83
barriers, to success, 2, 4–7, 119
Bennett, Elizabeth, 19–20, 81–82, 126, 141–43
Blink, 38
bootstrapping, 98
Bow Wow Buddies Foundation, 79–80, 155
bragging, 121
Branson, Richard, 41
Brittingham, Jean, 75–76, 124, 140
Brizendine, Louann, 6

Cambridge Innovation Center, 103
Camp Bow Wow, 47, 78, 154–55
capital, stages of, 90
Capitalism as if the World Matters, 3
Caretakers, 114
Center for Entrepreneurial Studies at Stanford University, 162
Champions, 114
Cheerleaders, 114
Chin, Ce Ce, 24, 51–52, 144–46
Collins, Tracey, 140
communication, 129–30
competitive matrix, creating, 67
corpus callosum, 42, 55
Covey, Steven, 84
Creativity, 16, 31–32, 41–46
crisis, economic. *See* economic crisis
crowd-funding, 99–100
Curiosity, 16–17, 31, 50–54
DailyCandy, 24, 145
debt financing. *See* funding options
Devine Color, 44, 112, 152–53
differences, between men and women, leveraging, 9
dominance, male. *See* sexism
Dream Dinners, 55–56, 88, 155–57
early-stage capital. *See* funding options
eBay Giving Works, 142
eBay, 142
economic: crisis, recent, 3; recovery, 4, 7–9

economy, caring, 3
economy, next. *See* next economy
ecosystem: entrepreneurial, 7–10; world, 2
Eisler, Riane, 3
Emotional Intelligence quotient, 7
empowerment, 128–30
EmpowHER, 21–23, 89, 143–44
entrepreneur, new definition of, 4, 25
equity funding. *See* funding options
expenses, estimating, 97
external strengths. *See also* Curiosity, Passion, Weaving, 16–17, 31, 59
failure, fear of, among women, 24–25, 88, 131–32
family, involving in business, 26, 91
Fashion Plates, 145, 149
FashionPlaytes.com, 25, 86, 148–50
fear of failure. *See* failure
feedback, 112–13
Feld, Brad, 94
finance models, 93
FOCUS, process, 18, 77–114
FUD factor, 89
funding options, 93–94: debt financing, 94; early-stage capital, 100–05; equity funding, 94; growth stage, 105–07; self-funding, 93, 98; start-up capital, 98–100
Ganahl, Heidi, 47, 78, 154–55
gender inequity. *See* sexism
Gladwell, Malcolm, 38
Golden Seeds, 106
Great Recession, 4
Grimmer, Neil, 87, 160–61
growth stage. *See* funding options
Hawken, Paul, 3

health. *See* self-care
Hill, Napoleon, 92
Hoffer, Jane, 65–68, 157–59
honesty, 118–22: radical, 118–21
Huang, Charles, 159
incubators, 103–04
Integrity, 16, 31–37
intention, 124–25
internal strengths. *See also* Creativity, Integrity, Intuition, 16, 31, 59
InternetRetailer.com, 149
Intuition, 16, 31–32, 37–41
investing: in other women-owned ventures, 138–39; style, of women, risk-averse, 92–93
Ishmael, 2
joint ventures, 104
Karma Physics, 153
King Robson, Michelle, 21–23, 89, 143–44
Kuna, Tina, 88, 156–57
language, new, of your business, 134
launch events, 114
Lechter, Michael, 94
Lechter, Sharon, 90, 93–94, 98, 162
Lerner, Gerda, 7
Listick, Barton, 158–59
loans: from friends/family, 99; local business-development, 105; personal, 101
longer-term strategic alliances, 104
Luther, Sara, 126, 141–43
Make Mine a Million, 103
Mass Challenge, 103
Mastermind Alliance, 92
McIlroy, Sarah, 25, 86, 148–50
Mendelson, Jason, 94
mentoring, 137–38

micro-lending, 101–02
MicroVentures, 101
Miller Paint Company, 44, 153
momentum, 139
"mommy track", 6
Mothers of Preschoolers, 156
Muslims, media bias toward, 150
Myers-Briggs Type Indicator (MBTI), 38
Napoleon Hill Foundation, 164
needs, business, identifying, 81
Nelson Bach, 146
Nest Collective, 87, 113, 159–62
nesting, 74–76
networking: in entrepreneurial groups, 72, 92; industry associations, joining, 72
next economy, 1–4
Niangi, 142
nondisclosure agreements, 96
O'Loughlin, Sheryl, 87, 113, 159–62
Ohanarama.com, 65–68, 157–59
OPM: Other People's Money, 94
Outwitting the Devil, 92, 164
Passion, 16–17, 31–32, 46–50
Past Interactions, 116–17
path to market, defining, 68–69
Pay Your Family First, 90, 162
paying it forward. *See* mentoring
peer-to-peer lending, 101–02
Pinchot, Libba, 84
Plum Organics, 87, 161
Porritt, Jonathon, 3
President's Advisory Council on Financial Literacy, 90
privilege, male. *See* sexism
Profounder, 101
Prosper.com, 101
"quick wins", 111–12

Quinn, Daniel, 2
recovery, economic. *See* economic recovery
responsibility, 122–23
Revolution Foods, 87, 160–61
Rich Dad, Poor Dad, 163
Rowling, J. K., 41
SCAN, process, 18, 64–76
scarcity mentality, 92
Schauffler, Gretchen, 44, 112, 152–53
self-care: emotional, 132; physical, 132–33
self-critical, tendency of women to be, 15
self-funding. *See* funding options
Seventh Generation, 146–47
sexism, 7, 13, 26, 119–20
Shade, Janice, 25, 39, 146–47
Sight & Sound, 162
Small Business Administration: loans, 102
SmartGirls Mirror, 10, 13–18, 27–28: interpreting, 29–62 *passim*
SmartGirls Way Methodology, 9, 13–18, 63. *See also* SCAN, FOCUS, THRIVE
stages, of business growth, 20, 22–23, 28–29
stakeholders: identifying, 71–72; reaching, 72–73
start-up capital. *See* funding options
stories, success: sharing yours, 136–37; from SmartGirls, 140–64
strength, 132
strengths, SmartGirls: interactions of, 60–61; optimizing, 60–61
support system, personal, 133–34
sustainability, 2
sustainable business, 84: schools

teaching, 84
sweat equity, 100
SWOT analysis, 73-74
talents, women's, unique, 13
Tareen, Amra, 111-12, 150-51
Tarr-Whelan, Linda, 7
TechStars Network, 103
The Female Brain, 6
The Real Wealth of Nations, 3
The Seven Habits of Highly Effective People, 84
Think and Grow Rich, 92
Three Feet from Gold, 164
THRIVE, 18
Time Together, 116-17
Tirrell, Mary Beth, 86, 149
TrueBody Products, 25, 39, 146-47
Trust Triangle, 116-17
trust, 115-18
Truth Telling, 116-18
Urban Outfitters, 145
values, 125-28
Venture Deals: Be Smarter than Your Lawyer and Venture Capitalist, 94
venture-capital, funding, 106-07
ViBI, articulating your, 20-23
Vidal, Gore, 139
Weaving, 16-17, 31-32, 54-58
win-win mentality, 83-84
woman's intuition, 37
womanly, ways of thinking and behaving, 1
Women Lead the Way, 7
women-owned businesses, social impact of, 1-2
work/life balance. *See* balance
Zuckerberg, Mark, 92

About the Authors

JEAN BRITTINGHAM

Jean Brittingham is the founder of SmartGirls Way and Brittingham Partners. Prior to starting SmartGirls Way, Jean worked with a diverse client group that included Fortune 100 companies, innovative start-ups, local and national governments, and nongovernmental organizations (NGOs). Jean has served on the Consumer Agenda Council of the World Economic Forum, as a strategic advisor and faculty member for the University of Cambridge Programme for Sustainability Leadership, and as an expert on gender equity for the Katerva Challenge, and sits on numerous business and nonprofit boards.

Her career in sustainable business has spanned over twenty years, ranging from the design of strategic collaborations to the implementation of programs across multiple sectors and businesses to promote and empower a sustainable future. While working as a consultant to some of the world's largest brands, Jean began to see a significant need for the unique views and attributes that women can bring to conversations, businesses, and economies. Fueled by her creativity, intuition, and passion, Jean established the SmartGirls Way and began creating the content—including a book uniquely focused on women's entrepreneurial strengths—to help rapidly scale the women's entrepreneurial movement that will form the critical base for the next economy.

TRACEY ANN COLLINS

Tracey Ann Collins is a writer and executive coach, specializing in women's leadership and organizational change management. She is a partner and Chief Creative Officer of the SmartGirls Way and also the founder and president of Mirror Group Consulting, which delivers content, coaching, and change-management services to clients in Europe and the United States.

Tracey began her career in journalism and communications and has spent over fifteen years working as a consultant to leaders of Fortune 500 and multinational organizations throughout Europe and the United States. Balancing the needs of her family and an international career led to seven moves in thirteen years and a crash course on adapting to new cultures and environments. During this time, she honed an intuitive ability to identify patterns and motivations behind challenging situations, a curiosity for people, and a passion for uncovering and sharing compelling stories. Tracey has been an honorary guest faculty member at the University of Erasmus, Rotterdam School of Management, and is an ongoing contributor to various magazines and change forums.